HUGO BLACK AND
THE BILL OF RIGHTS

HUGO BLACK

AND THE

BILL OF RIGHTS

PROCEEDINGS OF THE FIRST

HUGO BLACK SYMPOSIUM IN AMERICAN

HISTORY ON "THE BILL

OF RIGHTS AND AMERICAN DEMOCRACY"

edited by

Virginia Van der Veer Hamilton

Published for
The University of Alabama in Birmingham
by The University of Alabama Press
University, Alabama

LIBRARY OF CONGRESS CATALOGING IN PUBLICATION DATA

Hugo Black Symposium in American History, 1st,
  University of Alabama, 1976.
  Hugo Black and the Bill of Rights; proceedings of
the First Hugo Black Symposium in American History on
"The Bill of Rights and American Democracy".

  Includes index.
  1. Civil rights—United States—Congresses.
  2. Black, Hugo LaFayette, 1886-1971—Congresses.
  I. Hamilton, Virginia Van der Veer. II. Title.
  KF4749.A2H8 1976   342'.73'085   77-24689
  ISBN 0-8173-9309-9

CONTENTS

EDITOR AND CONTRIBUTORS

VIRGINIA VAN DER VEER HAMILTON is professor and chairperson of the Department of History at The University of Alabama in Birmingham, as well as coordinator of the annual Hugo Black Symposium in History sponsored by that institution. She received her A.B. and M.A. degrees from Birmingham-Southern College and her Ph.D. degree from The University of Alabama. She is the author of a number of articles as well as of two books, *Hugo Black: The Alabama Years* (1972) and *Alabama: A History* (1977).

WARREN EARL BURGER became Chief Justice of the United States in 1969. He was born in St. Paul, Minnesota, and received his A.B. degree from the University of Minnesota and his law degree from St. Paul College of Law (later Mitchell College of Law). He was admitted to the Minnesota bar in 1931 and was a member of the faculty at Mitchell College of Law from 1931 to 1948, after which he was in private law practice until 1953.

From 1953 to 1956, he served as Assistant Attorney General of the United States. In the period 1956–1969, he served as a member of the United States Court of Appeals in Washington, D.C. He has also served as Chancellor and Regent of the Smithsonian Institution, Honorary Chairman of the Institute of Judicial Administration, and on the boards of trustees of Mitchell College of Law, Macalester College, and the Mayo Foundation.

LEONARD W. LEVY is Andrew W. Mellon Professor of Humanities, and Chairperson of the Graduate Faculty of History at Claremont Colleges, Claremont, California. He is the author of numerous books on law and the Supreme Court, including *Against the Law: The Nixon Court and Criminal Justice*

(1974); *Judgments: Essays on Constitutional History* (1972); *Origins of the Fifth Amendment* (1968); *Jefferson and Civil Liberties: The Darker Side* (1963); and *Legacy of Suppression: Freedom of Speech and Press in Early American History* (rev. ed., 1973).

Professor Levy is also a general editor of *Major Crises in American History: Documentary Problems;* editor-in-chief of *The Bicentennial History of the American Revolution* and of *The American Heritage Series: A Documentary History of the United States,* and consulting editor on United States Constitutional History to the *Encyclopedia Britannica.* He is author of articles in the *Columbia Law Review, American Historical Review, Michigan Law Review, Boston University Law Review,* and other journals.

Professor Levy is a graduate of the Columbia University and, before becoming affiliated with the Claremont Colleges, was Earl Warren Professor of American Constitutional History at Brandeis University.

DONALD MEIKLEJOHN is Professor Emeritus of Philosophy and Social Sciences at Syracuse University. He is the author of articles on political philosophy, ethics, and education in philosophical journals and other learned journals, and of the book, *Freedom and the Public: Public and Private Morality in America* (1965). He has been a participant in the University of Chicago Round Table and other radio and television programs on current affairs.

Professor Meiklejohn received his A.B. degree from the University of Wisconsin and his Ph.D. degree in philosophy from Harvard University. He served during 1975–76 as resident chairperson of the Syracuse University Semester in Italy program. Before joining the Syracuse faculty in 1963, he taught at Dartmouth College, the College of William and Mary, and the University of Chicago. His current research interests lie in American political theory, focusing on the thought of Woodrow Wilson.

PAUL ABRAHAM FREUND is generally regarded as the nation's senior authority on the Supreme Court and constitutional law. He was appointed the first Carl M. Loeb University Professor at Harvard University in 1958. In 1968 he was elected a Senior Fellow of the Society of Fellows, a post which freed him to carry on his research and teaching in any part of the university. As Royal Professor of Law from 1957 to 1958, he occupied the oldest and most distinguished chair in the Harvard Law School.

Professor Freund is editor-in-chief of a projected eight-volume *History of the Supreme Court of the United States*, a project made possible by the will of the late Justice Oliver Wendell Holmes. He is author of *The Supreme Court of the United States*, published in 1961; *On Law and Justice*, published in 1968, and is coeditor with three of his Harvard colleagues of *Cases on Constitutional Law*.

A native of St. Louis, Missouri, Professor Freund received the A.B. degree from Washington University, St. Louis, Missouri; the LL.B. and the S.J.D. degrees from Harvard University. He was law clerk to the late Justice Louis D. Brandeis in 1932–33 and served in the Office of the Solicitor General, where he helped prepare the Government's arguments for the Supreme Court. As one of the University Professors at Harvard, Professor Freund has been a member of a small group of distinguished scholars "who are free to work on the frontiers of knowledge."

MAX LERNER is Professor Emeritus of American Civilization and World Politics at Brandeis University and a noted author whose columns are published in numerous newspapers and periodicals.

He received his A.B. degree at Yale University, his M.A. degree at Washington University (St. Louis, Missouri), and his Ph.D. degree from Robert Brookings Graduate School of

Economics and Government. Dr. Lerner has taught at Sarah Lawrence College, Harvard University, Williams College, as well as at the University of Delhi.

In addition to his academic career, Dr. Lerner has also served as managing editor of the *Encyclopaedia of Social Sciences*, editor of the *Nation*, and as a columnist for the New York *Star*. He is the author of numerous books, including *Ideas are Weapons* (1939), *The Mind and Faith of Justice Holmes* (1943), *America as a Civilization* (1957), and *Tocqueville and American Civilization* (1966).

ACKNOWLEDGMENTS

The Bicentennial Committee of The University of Alabama in Birmingham is indebted to numerous persons and organizations for assistance in the presentation of the first Hugo Black Symposium in History. Dr. Joseph F. Volker, then President of this University and now Chancellor of The University of Alabama System, and his fellow administrative officials gave the Bicentennial Committee full and enthusiastic support. The Committee received a supplemental grant from the Alabama Committee on the Humanities and Public Policy. Other contributors to the financial support of the symposium were the Student Government Association and the Graduate Student Association of University College.

Dean Donald E. Corley and members of the faculty of Cumberland School of Law, Samford University, collaborated with the Committee in the presentation of a session by former law clerks of Justice Black. Members of the Faculty Women's Club of The University of Alabama in Birmingham handled reservations for the Books and Authors Luncheon. Jerome A. Cooper, the first law clerk to Justice Black, made arrangements for a social gathering of former clerks and of persons involved with the symposium. Members of Sigma Delta Kappa Law Fraternity of the Birmingham School of Law contributed their services as ushers for the lectures.

The Committee is also indebted to those who presided at sessions of the symposium, including President Volker; Howell T. Heflin, then Chief Justice of the Alabama Supreme Court; the Honorable Seybourn H. Lynne, senior judge, United States District Court, Northern District of Alabama; and Judge Thomas S. Lawson, supernumerary justice, Supreme Court of Alabama. John Lamkin, assistant to the President of The University of Alabama in Birmingham, presided at the luncheon.

The final event of the symposium was the dedication of the site of the proposed Hugo Black Memorial Library at Ashland, Alabama. The people of Ashland, under the leadership of Morland Flegel, president of the Trustees of the Hugo Black Library, were hosts at a luncheon and a concert of Sacred Harp Singing preceding the dedication.

Finally, the Committee wishes to express its gratitude to members of the family of Justice Black, especially to Mrs. Hugo L. Black and Hugo Black, Jr., who came from over the state and nation to be present for this symposium.

PREFACE

On February 27, 1976, The University of Alabama in Birmingham observed the Bicentennial of the United States of America and the ninetieth anniversary of the birth of Hugo La Fayette Black. Justice Black, who emerged from an obscure farm community in the Alabama Piedmont to become a giant in the annals of the United States Supreme Court, was an appropriate focal figure for a symposium concerned with "The Bill of Rights and American Democracy." In thirty-five years on the high court, from the Great Depression through the tumultous 1960s, Justice Black maintained his personal vigil over the Bill of Rights, always insisting that the guarantees of the first ten amendments were absolute and that the due process clause of the Fourteenth Amendment bound the states to guarantee *all* of these rights to their citizens.

The Bicentennial Committee of this University also wished to memorialize Hugo Black's roots in Alabama. Black was always proud—sometimes sentimental—about his simple Alabama origins. He never denied, disdained, nor betrayed them (although many fellow Alabamians thought to the contrary about the matter of betrayal). During the course of a lecture at the Law School of Columbia University in 1968, Justice Black digressed to describe his beginnings:

> I was born in a frontier farm in the hills of Alabama during the troublesome times of Reconstruction after the Civil War, and my early life was spent in plain country surroundings. There I became acquainted with the "short and simple annals of the poor" among plain folks who learned most of their law and sound philosophies from the country schools and churches. It is a long journey from a frontier farm house in the hills of Clay County, Alabama, to the United States Supreme Court, a fact which no one knows better than I.[1]

xiv   *Hamilton*

Black was a descendant of foot soldiers in one cause that
succeeded and in other causes that ended in failure. His Irish
forebears served under Robert Emmet who led rebels in a
futile battle for independence from England in 1779. His
American ancestors served under Francis Marion in the
swamps of Carolina during the American Revolution. His
great-grandfather came to Coweta County, Georgia, on the
cutting edge of the Southern frontier, in 1827 to claim bounty
lands which he had won as a Revolutionary soldier. His
grandfather migrated west to Alabama to settle in the hills and
coves where Creek Indians had roamed before relentless white
settlers drove them west of the Mississippi.

Thus Hugo Black was a genuine product of the white farm
folk who constituted the majority of Alabama's population
during the nineteenth century. These Scotch-Irish pioneers
had poured into Alabama after the defeat of the Creeks at
Horseshoe Bend in 1814. They settled the Appalachian foot-
hills and piedmont, cleared forests with their axes, and planted
corn and cotton in infertile soil. Although they owned few
slaves, if any, most of these farmers flocked to the Confederate
colors. Black's uncle fought under Robert E. Lee at Gettys-
burg; his father ran away from home at fourteen to join the
ranks of the Confederacy. As an impressionable boy, Black
witnessed the tumult of Populism as farmers and industrial
laborers sought unsuccessfully to wrest political control from
the coalition of Birmingham industrialists and Black Belt plant-
ers, which had dominated the state since the end of Recon-
struction.

Hugo Black left Clay County to enroll as a student at Birmingham Medical College, a forerunner of The University of
Alabama Medical Center. One year's first-hand experience
convinced him that medicine was not his calling. After completing the two-year course of The University of Alabama
School of Law in Tuscaloosa, he returned to Birmingham to
seek clients in this raw, young steel city of the New South

where white migrants from the hill country and southern Europe competed with blacks from the Black Belt for jobs in steel mills and coal mines. During the 1920s, plain white working people, like the Populists before them, sought political power. This time they united in the dark and secret rites of the Ku Klux Klan, an authentic expression of their passions, prejudices, fears, and ambitions. In 1926, they achieved their first substantial victories in Alabama politics, choosing, among others, Hugo Black, the laboring man's lawyer, to represent them in the United States Senate. In order to win this office, Black had paid the price of affiliating with the Klan, a price which sensation-seekers and the sanctimonious never let him forget.

But it also should not be forgotten that Senator Black became an eloquent and consistent spokesman for the legitimate aspirations of his people—and of other plain Americans. He risked his seat in the Senate to lead the fight for a Fair Labor Standards Act, a landmark in the struggle of American workingmen for a living wage and a tolerable work week. In many ways a man ahead of his time, Senator Black called upon the federal government in the 1930s to commit itself not only to the shorter work week, the minimum wage, and the abolition of child labor, but also to health insurance, decent housing, a permanent work program for young Americans, and to federal aid to education so that sons and daughters of plain Americans might escape—as he had escaped—the bondage of ignorance and prejudice.

Like his Scotch-Irish ancestors, Hugo Black was a fighter. Using the power of the Senate to investigate, he exposed hidden lobbyists and big corporations that received special favors out of tax monies. At the start of the Great Depression, he fought against Herbert Hoover's concept that prosperity would trickle down from the top. Senator Black believed that prosperity woud rise upward from a well-paid, regularly employed labor force. He fought alongside President Franklin

Roosevelt in the unpopular and unsuccessful move to enlarge and thereby liberalize the Supreme Court. Alarmed by such ideas, established interests in Alabama were gearing to oppose his reelection when Hugo Black was nominated in 1937 to a seat on the Supreme Court.

Turner Catledge, who covered the United States Senate for the New York *Times* during the 1930s before moving up to become that newspaper's managing editor, observed the Alabama Senator perceptively:

> To be understood at all, [Black] had to be viewed in the light of his past. No man can come up whole and unscathed, by his own efforts only, from the prejudiced backwardness of the rural South . . . The long struggle had left its mark on Senator Black.[2]

A fellow Alabamian, born and reared in circumstances similar to those of Hugo Black, made an equally perceptive and even more prophetic comment. During the national furor over the suitability of a onetime Klan member on the Supreme Court, Judge E. E. Callaway wrote:

> I know Justice Black and I know he is neither a Klansman, Communist, nor Radical at heart, and if he lives he will prove to be a rational, progressive, constitutional American . . . the American people have no conception of the vicissitudes of adversity Justice Black had to overcome in his early life . . . He had to be a political genius to survive. This is what enabled him to navigate the destructive rapids of the political philosophy that had disgraced Alabama and the South since the Civil War, and gave him the opportunity which he now has to prove himself a great American.[3]

But allow Hugo Black himself to have the last word. Fighting in 1930 to defeat Herbert Hoover's nomination of a railroad attorney to a seat on the Interstate Commerce Commission, Senator Black told the Senate:

> Show me the kind of steps a man made in the sand five years ago, and I will show you the kind of steps he is likely to make in the same sand five years hence.[4]

Hugo Black's steps during his long Court career follow the direction set in his Senate years. They led toward equal justice for plain Americans; they are embedded, not in shifting sand, but in enduring law.

VIRGINIA VAN DER VEER HAMILTON

NOTES

1. Hugo L. Black, Carpentier Lectures, Columbia University Law School, New York, N.Y., March 23, 1968.
2. Joseph Alsop and Turner Catledge, *The 168 Days* (New York: Doubleday, Doran and Co., 1938), p. 301.
3. E. E. Callaway, "Notes on a Kleagle," *American Mercury* (February 1938) XLIII, 248–49.
4. *Congressional Record*, 71st Cong., 2nd Sess., 3353–4005.

HUGO BLACK AND
THE BILL OF RIGHTS

Dedicatory Address

Warren E. Burger

PROFESSOR FREUND REFERRED TO "THE UNTIDINESS OF JUDICIAL decision." Of course, he was not using those terms in a disparaging sense but rather reflecting that judicial decisions necessarily reflect lack of symmetry in what they deal with. In short, that is the very "nature of the beast." From many occasions of talking with him and having read, I think, almost everything he has ever written, I know that is what he means. I think he would agree with me that if we ever have a time when all nine on the Supreme Court of the United States agree on everything, that would be the time for the people of this country to worry about their freedoms. And, of course, nothing characterized Hugo Black more than his passionate advocacy and his respect for those who had different views.

Something Professor Freund said gave me this thought—and it might be good as the dedicatory line for this occasion—that if all 101 men who have been and now are on the Supreme Court of the United States agreed unanimously on restricting some exercise of religion in the area he was discussing tonight, Justice Black, I suspect, would say the unanimous opinion of 101 Justices of the Supreme Court from 1790 to the present time could not drive any man's God out of any place that men and women want that God to be. And so the course of dealing with the religion clauses under our system is bound to "zig" a

little and "zag" a little, which means it will never be frozen.
There will never be any established church and there will
never be any prohibition of the free excercise of religion "while
the Court sits."

The sponsors of the program agreed that I could come here
tonight, not to give formal address or speech, but to reminisce
informally with you about Hugo Black, the flesh and blood
man. No man can occupy the position that he did, beginning
with his early career in politics in this state and as one of its
outstanding lawyers, then to go on to the United States Senate, and to the Supreme Court for substantially as long as John
Marshall and Roger Taney, and only slightly short of the
tenure of William O. Douglas, and not become something of a
legend. The image that is created by the media and other
processes in our modern society tends really to dehumanize.
Let me tell you, if you will bear with me, a few things about
my personal day-to-day relations with Hugo Black and some
anecdotes about him.

Hugo Black had no occasion to remember the first time I
met him. It was, I think, 1938 or 1939, a few years after he
had gone on the Court, and as was his habit through his entire
career, he spent the entire summer in Washington. He was
studying, reading in history and philosophy, and preparing
for the Fall Term. He was at the Court almost every day.

As a young lawyer, I was in Washington on business for
my law firm and decided to spend two or three days in the
Supreme Court library preparing a brief in a very difficult tax
case. Some routine motion was involved that required an
order to be signed. I went to the Clerk and he said, "Mr.
Justice Black is here. I will take you in." I had assumed that I
would leave the order to be signed by a Justice. The Clerk
escorted me to Justice Black's office, where in these later years
I spent many, many happy hours in private discussions and
conferences. I explained the matter and he wanted to know
what kind of case it was. I said, "a tax case rising out of the

Minnesota statutes." His face fell a little bit because, I think, he felt about tax cases as Justice Douglas has often expressed, "they involve nothing but money." He signed the order.

When I reminded him of the 1938 occasion, it was not possible for him to remember it, but it made a very vivid impression on me as a young man being received by a Justice of the Court with great cordiality and friendliness.

The next time I saw Hugo Black I was standing at the lectern, much like the one we have here, arguing a case in the Supreme Court in the early 1950s. On one occasion I felt the vigor of his advocacy and his attitudes because in the 1950s Justice Black was in his physical prime, his mental prime, and the prime vigor of his beliefs. I was arguing a case for the United States that was very unsympathetic. As a member of the Eisenhower administration, I was trying to defend an executive order of President Truman relating to the employee security program. You will remember that 1954 was on the edge of the "McCarthy Era." Justice Black used his trial court techniques and leaned across the bench after I had been making a point about an opinion he had written in the case of *Williams v. New York*, familiar I'm sure to all the lawyers and judges here. I had apparently pushed it a little bit too much, and he leaned over the bench and said, "I don't see why you seem to get so much comfort out of what I said in the *Williams* case." He didn't say it quite that gently, and he had his finger wagging in my direction. I responded not only that I took comfort, but also that his opinion was dispositive of the instant case unless he had changed his mind. He got rather red in the face, and as the dialogue continued, he pressed me very vigorously. I said in essence:

Mr. Justice Black, in *Williams v. New York*, you wrote that a judge of the New York state courts could decide whether to send a man to the electric chair for a very brutal murder rather than sending him to prison for life. You held that the state

judge alone, one judge, could make the decision between sen-
tencing him to life imprisonment or sending him to the electric chair on the basis of a private pre-sentence report made by
the probation officer which was never revealed to the defendant, and he had come to this Court claiming that was a denial
of due process because these were unknown informants.

Justice Black pursued the discussion vigorously, and in sub-
stance I responded: "If, as you said then, a man could be sent
to the electric chair on that kind of information, I submit that
the government can rely on that kind of information to dismiss
a nontenured government employee." Justice Black was not
overly happy with my point, and since I was arguing a very
unsympathetic case, I was not too happy either.

It happened that one of Justice Black's former law clerks,
Melford Cleveland of Alabama, applied for a position in the
Department of Justice while I was Assistant Attorney General. I appointed him and we became acquainted. He wanted
me to become better acquainted with Justice Black, and after I
went on the Court of Appeals in 1956, he arranged for the
three of us to have lunch; that led to a series of lunches with
Justice Black. I would also meet him from time to time at
social gatherings and receptions; occasionally he would draw
me aside and say, "I read your dissent in such and such a case
and I'm not sure I agree with it but stick to it—stick to it.
Dissent is what keeps everybody in our business on his toes."

This, I think, in many respects expresses an aspect of Justice Black that many people missed, simply because he was
such a passionate advocate for whatever he believed; he was
also a good listener and a respecter of the views of others.

From the close intimacy with Justice Black during my early
years on the Supreme Court I can speak of the unfolding
relationship built on nearly fifteen years prior acquaintance.
In the Supreme Court the relationships among the Justices are
more intimate probably than in a law firm or on the faculty of

a university. In the Supreme Court of the United States, little is done without the participation of all nine Justices. And so we live in intimate contact with each other that is hard for people outside to understand. We are necessarily walled in, partly because we are so enormously busy and partly because we are focusing constantly on the problems that are being presented to us.

After the former law clerk of Justice Black's brought us together, our friendship grew through occasional luncheons. I told him I had heard of his program of reading the classics, history, and philosophy. I reminded him that I had never gone to college in the traditional or conventional sense; that I had gone to the University of Minnesota at night for four years and then four years to night law school, and I was aware of great gaps in my education. He gave me a reading list and occasionally we would talk about some of the subjects. Sometimes it would appear that we did not agree on a particular point of view. I remember responding to him once: yes, I had read it, but I did not think I read the author in exactly the same way he did.

In the summer of 1969, when I came on the Court, I had then been on the Court of Appeals for more than thirteen years and had some acquaintance with the Supreme Court Justices. Nevertheless I did not have an intimate acquaintance with the internal procedures and machinery of the Court. As new matters would come up, I would walk to his Chambers and consult him; he could not have been more generous and helpful in guiding me and getting acquainted with the work of the Court. All of the Justices had that relationship with him. Once he said something to the effect that, as men who had spent many days in courtrooms and in controversy, we had become professional in our capacity to disagree without becoming disagreeable about it.

He confirmed a story Justice Brennan told me which illustrates another side of him. Toward the end of a Term of Court

he and Justice Brennan were in strong disagreement over some
case, and Justice Brennan is as passionate an advocate as was
Hugo Black. Justice Brennan told me they had had many
conversations about the case and finally had one telephone conversation in an effort to reconcile their differences. Justice
Brennan said he used what he feared were unduly sharp remarks to Justice Black. A short time later, Justice Black
walked in his office, closed the door, sat down, and said: "Bill,
I want you to go home; I want you to get out of here. This
place is a pressure cooker, especially near the end of the Term.
You get out of here and go home and forget about this case and
I won't do anything on it until you get back." I've already
said—and others have said—that Justice Black was warm in
his personal attachments, as warm as he was vigorous in his
opposition or his advocacy. His friends could do very little
wrong, and yet he did not treat an adversary as not being able
to do anything right.

When I came to the Court as a "new broom," as every new
Chief Justice is bound to be, there were a number of things I
had observed that seemed to me were due for a change. Some
of them were small things, but they afford another view of the
human side of Hugo Black. The practice had been, from the
2nd of February 1790, when the Court first met, that anyone
admitted to the Supreme Court was required to be physically
in the Courtroom at the lectern with a sponsor after having
filed papers endorsed by two sponsors who were members of
the Bar. Some days the Court devoted an hour or even two
hours to this process, and I felt this was an enormous waste of
a valuable national resource in the form of the time of nine
Justices of the Court. It was a pleasant occasion for the
lawyers and for the spectators, but I thought the realities required something else. I proposed that the Supreme Court
amend its rules to conform with the rules of every State Supreme Court in the country and federal Appellate Courts that
lawyers could be admitted by filing the papers without ap-

pearing in the Court. Justice Black, as Senior Justice, had enormous standing with all of us, so there were not very many changes we could make if he wasn't willing at least to tolerate them. He pointed out that this was a great tradition of the Court and that it was a fine public relations exercise to have these lawyers come in. I reminded him that sometimes it was very expensive for a lawyer who had a case coming up to travel all the way from California or the Midwest in order to be admitted before he could begin to file papers. I bided my time until the end of the 1969 Term. In April or May of 1970 on one day, literally, there were more than five hundred lawyers presented for admission. They were all from Massachusetts and had come down in busloads. Senator Edward Kennedy of Massachusetts moved their admission. He had a list which he kept turning over, and I think he drank at least three glasses of water during the time he went through this ritual. It took several hours. These lawyers were brought into the Courtroom in platoons of a hundred. The Marshal would clear the Courtroom and then bring in another platoon of lawyers and wives and children of the lawyers. Nine Justices would sit, twiddling their thumbs, having informal conversations with each other for the ten or fifteen minutes it took for each platoon of a hundred or more lawyers to leave the Courtroom and another platoon to enter.

Shortly after that, over six hundred were presented by two Senators from a state. They took turns so that one Senator could rest his vocal cords while the other one was going through this very pleasant but time-consuming ritual. That day the admissions continued until about two o'clock in the afternoon. The following day at the Conference I proposed that we amend the rule as I had suggested. Justice Black protested less vigorously, and we finally compromised so as to permit lawyers to appear in the Courtroom for admission but allow others who wanted to be admitted on papers to do so. This resulted in most of the five or six thousand lawyers ad-

mitted each year taking advantage of the new procedure and
saving valuable time but preserving the tradition of a personal
appearance for those who desired.

Soon after this change I suggested that we could not justify
the expenditure of time to read opinions of the Court when
they were announced, and I advised my colleagues that on
opinion days I would not read my opinions or even summarize
them, but would merely say that for reasons stated in the
opinion filed with the Clerk, the judgment of the particular
court was affirmed or reversed. Justice Black argued that this
practice was a great tradition we ought to keep. I responded that
the pressures on our time were too great to warrant using
several hours a week—of nine Justices—simply to keep a tradition whose original purpose had disappeared. One Justice
within recent times not only read the opinion in full but read
most, if not all, the footnotes. Sometimes it would be two
o'clock in the afternoon before the Court began its business.
Today the Justices, at most, present an abbreviated version of
the opinion in less than five minutes.

Justice Black disagreed with one change I suggested, but
more in fun than anything else. For years the practice had
been for the Justices to have thirty minutes for lunch on argument days. The function of the Chief Justice requires him to
check in at his Chambers as soon as he gets off the bench to see
if a Circuit Chief Judge or the Director of the Administrative
Office had called about a problem, or whether some emer-
gency motion was being presented. As a result it would be
seven or eight minutes before I would get to the dining room,
and fifteen minutes later the buzzer would go off while I was
half finished with my lunch. Most of the other Justices didn't
like this pressure, so I proposed that we extend our lunch
period to sixty minutes. Justice Black's answer was, "You
fellows eat too much in thirty minutes; you'll kill yourselves
with your teeth if you have an hour." Then he would quote

Chief Justice Hughes, who had said that more men had killed themselves on this Court with overeating than with overwork.

Every day each Justice receives requests for autographs and many students who are autograph collectors enclose a card reading, "Will you please sign this." One student wrote in and said, "I'm 14 years old and in the 8th grade and I'm enclosing five cards. I want one for my collection and four to trade for an autograph of Justice Black." When I told Justice Black of that episode, he literally blushed and said, "No, you're pulling my leg." When I assured him I was serious, he replied: "Well, there's a reason for that. They've got a much longer time to get your autograph in the future than they have mine."

One of the other changes we made—a physical change—has some interesting sidelights. The bench of the Supreme Court, from the first time the Court sat in 1790, was a straight bench and the Justices sat in a straight line. When the new building was constructed, beginning in 1932, the bench remained the same. When I argued cases there, it was a common experience to have a Justice on one side ask a question at the same time another Justice was asking a question, and perhaps even a third Justice. Even after Chief Justice Warren put in new amplifying equipment and acoustical treatment, the Justices couldn't always hear each other. I proposed that we modify the bench to conform with the practice which has been in vogue for the past thirty or thirty-five years—an eliptical-shaped bench. I arranged to have a scale model made so that the Justices could make a judgment on a physical setting rather than on a blueprint. The Capitol Architect, who controls our building, made the diagram and a cabinetmaker constructed a plywood mock-up that was an exact replica of the bench. We placed this replica in a large conference room of the Court, on a platform exactly the same distance off the floor as in the main Courtroom. The bench was originally made in three sections, and all the cabinetmaker had to do was simply separate the parts and bring the two outer sections forward. The regular chairs were all placed back of the model bench, and the discussion was all in favor of the change. Justice Harlan, who was one of the great appellate advocates of this country before he came on the Court, said: "I would like to go out and take a look from the lawyer's point of view." He did so, and from the lectern engaged in a colloquy, much as Justices do with lawyers arguing a case. Finally, he said, "Well, I'm quite impressed with it and I like it, but there's one thing that's very bad about it." Although his eyes were failing, I could see a twinkle in them, because he was only about eight feet in front of us. One Justice said: "What's the problem, John?" He answered: "It's good in every respect except one, and that is that it gives an inordinate position of dignity and prominence to the three men sitting in the center section." Hugo Black's hand went up immediately, and then he said, in that beautiful soft voice: "John, you never were more wrong in your life. It isn't discriminatory; what you see is just the natural consequence of the distinction of the three men sitting here."

I mentioned Justice Black's reading list, and after his death I spoke to Mrs. Black and to Mr. Hugo, Jr., and other members of his family and suggested that a library of this sort was a great treasure house for scholars and historians, partly because of the marginal notes he had made. He would write, "I don't agree" or "I agree" or "Yes," or if he needed more space he'd go to the margin and write his own reaction there or in the back of the book. I suggested we would provide a Hugo Black reading room in the Supreme Court if those books could be placed there to be available to any scholar under the supervision of our library staff. That plan was carried out; those books are now in the library and constitute a permanent memorial to this remarkable man from Alabama. I find that my law clerks drop into the Hugo Black reading room, peruse these books, and sometimes make copies of the list for their future use. I believe this reading room will influence many people in the years ahead.

Mr. President, to you and to the members of the faculty and the governing board of the University and to the members of the Black family and his friends, I close by repeating that I am honored to dedicate this Symposium to Hugo Black, who was not only a friend and a colleague, but a teacher, and our years of relationship and work together have made a permanent impression on me. I hope that the State of Alabama and the South will continue to enlarge their understanding and appreciation of this remarkable man.

History and Judicial History:
The Case of the Fifth Amendment

Leonard W. Levy

BY NOW WE ALL KNOW THE NOTORIOUS FACT: THE SUPREME
Court has flunked history. The justices stand censured for
abusing historical evidence in a way that reflects adversely on
their intellectual rectitude as well as on their historical competence. They frequently use "law office history," which is a
function of advocacy. The Court artfully selects historical
facts from one side only, ignoring contrary data, in order to
give the appearance of respectability to judgments resting on
other grounds. Alfred H. Kelly showed that the Court's historical scholarship is simplistic, manipulative, and devoid of
impartiality. He referred to the Court's "historical felony,"
"mangled constitutional history," and the confusion of the
writing of briefs with the writing of history.

Ever since Charles Fairman demolished Justice Black's opinion in the Adamson case on the question whether the Fourteenth Amendment was intended to incorporate the Bill of
Rights, scholars have criticized the Court's use of history.
Alexander Bickel negated the Court's reading of the history of
the Fourteenth Amendment on the question of racial segregation. I disproved the Court's assertion that the First Amendment was intended to supersede the common law of seditious
libel. The Court's use of history in cases on the Fifth Amend-

ment's self-incrimination clause also fits a pattern of historical incompetence and law-office history.

The most historically minded opinion on the Fifth Amendment was Justice Moody's in *Twining v. New Jersey*, decided in 1908. *Twining*, which the Court abandoned in 1964, runs counter to the general trend of decisions favoring a liberal construction of the Fifth Amendment. But the Court's use of history in *Twining* is representative of its historical knowledge. The question was whether the right against self-incrimination was "a fundamental principle of liberty and justice which inheres in the very idea of free government" and therefore ought to be included within the concept of due process of law safeguarded from state abridgment. Relying on its version of history, the Court decided against the right. Justice Moody said that he had resorted to "every historical test by which the meaning of the phrase [of the Fifth Amendment] can be tried." The 1637 trial of Anne Hutchinson proved, he alleged, that the Massachusetts authorities were "not aware of any privilege against self-incrimination or any duty to respect it." Justice Black, in his famous Adamson dissent, in effect exclaimed, "Of course not," because the court that tried Anne Hutchinson for heresy, believing that its religious convictions must be forced upon others, could not believe that dissenters had any rights worth respecting. But, incriminating interrogation was routine in 1637 on both sides of the Atlantic in criminal cases. Nevertheless the Hutchinson case could not reveal whether the judges were aware of the right against self-incrimination or of a duty to respect, because she did not claim it. She welcomed incriminating questions as an opportunity to reveal God's word as she saw it; she freely and voluntarily incriminated herself. Justice Moody did not know that in 1637 the same Massachusetts court, when put on the defensive by objections to its procedure and questioning, explained that it did not seek to examine the defendant by compulsory means, by using an incriminating oath, nor seek to "draw matter from him whereupon to proceed against him." The maxim *nemo tenetur seipsum prodere*—no one is bound to accuse himself— was widely known among the Massachusetts Puritans.

Moody said in *Twining* that the right was not in Magna Carta and that the practice of self-incriminatory examinations had continued for more than four centuries after 1215. That was short of the whole truth. As early as 1246, when the church introduced its inquisitorial oath-procedure into England, a procedure that required self-incrimination, Henry III condemned it as "repugnant to the ancient Customs of his Realm" and to "his peoples Liberties." In the fourteenth century Parliament outlawed the church's incriminatory oath-procedure, and when the King's Council emulated that procedure, Parliament protested and reenacted section 29 of Magna Carta. One such reenactment, in 1354, for the first time used the phrase "by due process of law," and seen in its context that great statute condemned incriminating examinations, when conducted outside the common-law courts, as violations of Magna Carta or denials of due process. In *Twining* the Supreme Court failed to recognize that Magna Carta grew in meaning and became the symbol and source of the expanding liberties of the subject. Thus, in 1590 Robert Beale, the clerk of the Privy Council, declared that "by the Statute of Magna Carta and the olde lawes of this realme, this oathe for a man to accuse himself was and is utterlie inhibited." This became the view of other common-lawyers, of Chief Justice Edward Coke, and of Parliament. To allege that Magna Carta did not outlaw compulsory self-incrimination was to rest on its meaning in 1215, not on what it came to mean. The *Twining* Court was wrong too when declaring that the Petition of Right of 1628 did not address itself to the evil of compulsory self-incrimination. It did, in the passage censuring "an oath . . . not warrantable by the laws or statutes of this realm. . . ." That oath, which preceded interrogation, operated to coerce confessions.

The Court in *Twining* also found significance in the fact that compulsory self-incrimination was not condemned by the Stamp Act Congress, the Continental Congress, or the Northwest Ordinance. But the Stamp Act Congress mentioned only trial by jury among the many well-established rights of the criminally accused; failure to enumerate them all proved nothing. The Court failed to note that the Continental Congress did claim that the colonists were "entitled to the common law of England," which had long protected the right against self-incrimination, nor did the Court note, or know, that Congress in 1778, in an investigation of its own, did respect that right when a witness claimed it. The Northwest Ordinance did contain a guarantee of "judicial proceedings according to the course of the common law." Indeed, the Supreme Court itself said in *Twining* that by 1776 courts recognized the right even in the states whose constitutions did not protect it. Justice Moody mentioned six states whose constitutions did provide such protection, but there were eight. What Moody did not recognize was that every state that had a separate bill of rights protected the right against self-incrimination. He noted that only four of the original thirteen states insisted that the right be incorporated in the new United States Constitution, but he failed to note that these were the only states which ratified the Constitution with recommendations for a national bill of rights. Using Moody's yardstick, one could argue that the fundamental concept of due process of law was not fundamental at all because it did not appear in any of the thirteen state constitutions and was recommended by only one state ratifying convention. Moody remarked that the principle that no person could be compelled to be a witness against himself "distinguished the common law from all other systems of jurisprudence." Since the principle was first elevated to constitutional status in America, and since it was safeguarded by every state having a bill of rights, and since it fit the several definitions of due process that Moody offered, there is no explaining the Court's finding that the right came into existence as a mere rule of evidence that was not "an essential part of due process." *Twining* was founded on inaccurate and insufficient data. Contrary to the Court's assertion, the right against self-incrimination did evolve as an essential part of due process and as a fundamental principle of liberty and justice. Thus, Ben Franklin in 1735 called it a natural right ("the common Right of Mankind"), and Baron Geoffrey Gilbert, the foremost English authority on evidence at the time, called it part of the "Law of Nature."

Other cases reveal the justices to be equally inept as historians even when conscripting the past into service for the defense and expansion of the Fifth Amendment. The most historically minded opinion of this kind was Justice Douglas's dissent in *Ullmann v. United States*, decided in 1956. The seven-man majority, speaking through Justice Frankfurter, sustained the constitutionality of Congress's Immunity Act of 1954. That act required that in certain cases involving national security, a federal court might require a witness to testify or produce records that might incriminate him, on condition that his revelations could not be used as evidence against him in any criminal proceeding. Frankfurter's opinion for the majority stressed the importance of history in interpreting the Fifth. History, he said, showed that it should be construed broadly, though he construed it narrowly. Frankfurter observed that, "the privilege against self-incrimination is a specific provision of which it is peculiarly true that 'a page of history is worth a volume of logic.'" But Frankfurter did not provide that page of history. He offered only the brief platitude that the Fifth was aimed against a recurrence of the Inquisition and of the Star Chamber. Though Frankfurter was the most historically minded scholar on the Court, he was apparently unaware of the several colonial precedents in support of his argument that the right cannot be claimed if the legal peril, which is the reason for its existence, ceases.

Douglas's dissent, in which Black joined, is a splendid specimen of law-office history; most of his history was not even relevant to his conclusion that the Immunity Act violated the Fifth Amendment. Douglas's relevant history, which dealt with the concept of infamy, was unsound. He claimed that the act was unconstitutional because it was not broad enough: it did not protect against infamy or public disgrace. In support of this proposition he had to prove that the framers of the Fifth meant it to protect against disclosures resulting in public disgrace. Such evidence as history provided to support his proposition was unknown to Douglas. His evidence was far-fetched, for he based his argument on the fact that protection against infamy is found in the ideas of Beccaria and the *Encyclopedistes* whom Jefferson read. But the Fifth Amendment was exclusively the product of English history and American colonial experience. The influence of Continental theorists was nonexistent. As for Jefferson, he had nothing to do with the making of the Fifth. Indeed, he omitted protections against self-incrimination in the two model constitutions that he proposed for Virginia.

Douglas's other evidence dealt not with the issue in question, immunity, but with the general origins of the Fifth. He referred to the Puritan hatred of the self-incriminatory oath ex officio used by the Star Chamber and its ecclesiastical counterpart, the High Commission. The hatred existed, but there were significant differences between the Star Chamber's use of the oath and the High Commission's. The High Commission required the suspect to take that oath to tell the truth as the first step of the examination, and then interrogated him orally without telling him the charges against him or the identity of his accusers. By contrast, the Star Chamber normally provided a bill of complaint, as specific as common-law indictment, and permitted the accused to have plenty of time to answer the charges in writing and with the advice of counsel; only then did the accused have to take the oath and be orally interrogated. The maxim *nemo tenetur seipsum prodere*, from which the right against self-incrimination derived, did not operate in the High Commission, but the Star Chamber respected the maxim. Accordingly the common lawyers who supported that maxim and assaulted the oath ex officio, did not attack the use of the oath by the Star Chamber. Too often the Star Chamber is identified as the symbol of inquisitional procedure, the opposition to which gave rise to the right against self-incrimination. Thus Justice Black in his *Adamson* dissent spoke loosely of the Star Chamber practice of compelling people to testify against themselves, and the same thought is in Chief Justice Warren's opinion for the Court in the *Miranda* case which extended the right against self-incrimination to the police station.

Black in *Adamson*, Douglas in *Ullmann*, and Warren in *Miranda* referred to John Lilburne's Star Chamber trial of 1637 and his refusal to take the oath. As these justices imply, Lilburne was more responsible than any other single individual for the recognition by the common-law courts of the right against self-incrimination, but not because of Lilburne's opposition to the oath in 1637. In that case the Star Chamber had abandoned its normal procedure by demanding the oath first instead of providing the written complaint first; so, Lilburne refused the oath, the first—he said—ever to have done so before the Star Chamber—proof that its procedure in 1637 was exceptional. Justice Douglas should have quoted later statements by Lilburne when tried by common-law courts in the 1640s that even in the absence of the oath and after common-law indictment, Magna Carta and the Petition of Right protected a man from being examined on interrogatories concerning himself—"concerning," which is far broader than "incriminating." At his treason trial in 1649 Lilburne placed the right against self-incrimination squarely in the context of what he called "fair play," "fair trial," "the due process of the law," and "the good old laws of England." Justice Douglas gave to John Lilburne a page of his opinion in *Ullmann*, straining the evidence and never knowing that history provided him with stronger facts with which to construct his one-sided argument.

Douglas's *Ullmann* opinion distorted the evidence concerning an important episode in the colonial history of the right against self-incrimination. He mentioned that Governor Bradford of Plymouth sought the advice of his ministers on the question, "How farr a magistrate may extracte a confession from a delinquente, to acuse himselfe of a capitall crime, seeing *Nemo tenetur prodere seipsum.*" Inexplicably, Douglas omitted the Latin phrase that both supported his argument and invalidated the generalization in *Twining*, based on the Anne Hutchinson case, that the right against self-incrimination was then unknown. Three Plymouth ministers, Douglas said, were unanimous in concluding that the oath was illegal, and he quoted as "typical" only the answer of Ralph Patrich that the magistrate might not extract a confession "by any violent means," whether by oath or "punishment." Douglas concealed the answer of Charles Chauncy who said, "But now, if the question be mente of inflicting bodly torments to extract a confession from a mallefactor, I conceive that in matters of highest consequence, such as doe conceirne the saftie or runie of states of countries, magistrates may proceede so farr to bodily torments, as racks and hote-irons to extracte a confession, espetially wher presumptions are strounge; but otherwise by no means."

Chauncy would not force self-incrimination by oath, but he would employ torture to coerce confessions in matters such as sedition or treason and perhaps heresy. Douglas's account omitted Chauncy and omitted the fact that Governor Winthrop, who received the opinions of the elders and magistrates of Massachusetts Bay, New Haven, and Connecticut, as well as of Plymouth, recorded that "most" answered that in a capital case if one witness or "strong presumptions" pointed to the suspect, the judge could examine him "strictly," and "he is bound to answer directly, though to the peril of this life." History is not a judicial strong point, but judges must look at the text as well as at history.

What illumination is available from the face of the Fifth? Its words include more than merely a right against self-incrimination, which is a phrase of modern origin. The clause in the Fifth is, "no person . . . shall be compelled in any criminal case to be a witness against himself." That formulation protects against more than just compulsory self-incrimination. A person can be a witness against himself in ways that do not incriminate him. He may, in a criminal case, injure his civil interests or disgrace himself in the public mind. Thus the Fifth could be construed on its face to protect against disclosures that expose one to either civil liability or infamy. The Fifth could also be construed to protect an ordinary witness as well as the criminal defendant himself, for it applies to any person.

On the other hand, the clause is restricted on its face to criminal cases. The phrase "criminal case" seems to some to exclude civil cases. Also, to some judges no criminal case exists until a formal charge has been made against the accused. Under such an interpretation the right would have no existence until the accused is put on trial; before that, when he is taken into custody, interrogated by the police, or examined by a grand jury, he would not have the benefit of the right. Nor would he have its benefit in a nonjudicial proceeding like a legislative investigation or an administrative hearing. The Supreme Court has given the impression that the clause, if taken literally, does have restrictive effects. But the Court refuses to take the clause literally. Of no other clause in the Constitution has the Court declared that it cannot mean what it seems to say. Thus, in *Counselman v. Hitchcock*, a major case on the Fifth decided in 1892, the Court held that the Fifth did protect ordinary witnesses, even in federal grand-jury proceedings. Unanimously the Court declared, "It is impossible that the meaning of the constitutional provision can only be that a person shall not be compelled to be a witness against himself in a criminal prosecution against himself." Although the Court did not explain why it was "impossible," the Court was right. Had the framers of the Fifth intended the literal, restrictive meaning, then their constitutional provision would have been a meaningless gesture because there was no need in the eighteenth century to protect the accused at his trial: he was not permitted to give testimony, whether for or against himself, at the time of the framing of the Fifth. Making the criminal defendant competent to be a witness in his own case, if he wanted to, was a reform of the late nineteenth century.

The Court has construed the clause as if its framers neither meant what they said nor said what they meant. Generally the Court has acted as if the letter killeth. Seeking the spirit and policy of the Fifth, the Court has, on the whole, given it a liberal interpretation, on the principle that "it is as broad as the mischief against which it seeks to guard." In effect the Court has taken the position that the Fifth embodied the still evolving common law of the matter, rather than a precise rule of fixed meaning. In so doing the Court has been true to the intent of the framers of the Fifth and to its historical meaning. The Court, in its liberal interpretations, has had the past on its side, but has not known it. Many apparent innovations are supported by old practices and precedents. Those who do not know history are doomed to repeat it.

What, briefly, does history reveal about the scope and meaning of the Fifth? First, its framers meant to bequeath a large and still-growing principle.

Second, the right did extend to grand-jury proceedings, as early as the seventeenth century.

Third, the right extended to witnesses that early too.

Fourth, the right extended to both witnesses and parties in civil as well as criminal cases if a truthful answer to a question might result in a forfeiture, penalty, or criminal prosecution. The proof consists of many early English and American decisions. In a little-known aspect of the famous case of *Marbury v. Madison*, Chief Justice Marshall asked the Attorney General of the United States, Levi Lincoln, what he had done with Marbury's missing commission which Lincoln had had in his possession when serving as acting secretary of state. The Attorney General, who probably had burned the commission, refused to incriminate himself by answering, and the Supreme Court sustained him, though he was a witness in a civil suit.

Fifth, there are many early state cases showing that neither witnesses nor parties were required to answer against themselves if to do so would expose them to public disgrace or infamy. The origins of so broad a right of silence can be traced as far back as sixteenth-century claims by Protestant reformers like William Tyndale and Thomas Cartwright in connection with their argument that no man should be compelled to accuse himself—or to shame himself. The idea passed to the common lawyers, including Coke, was accepted even in the Star Chamber as well as English case-law, and found expression in Blackstone and the American manuals of practice. Yet the Supreme Court restricted the scope of the historical right when ruling that the Fifth did not protect against compulsory self-disgrace. Its decision to that effect in 1896 was oblivious to the history of the matter. In the 1956 *Ullmann* case reaffirming that precedent of 1896, Frankfurter for the Court stressed the importance of history, yet offered none, and, forgetting that the Constitution does not speak of merely a stunted privilege against self-incrimination, alleged that the "sole concern [of the privilege against self-incrimination] as its name indicates [!] is with the danger of giving testimony leading to the infliction of criminal penalities." History was on the side of Douglas and Black, dissenting, with respect to the question whether the "privilege" embraced public infamy, but they did not know it.

Sixth, from the standpoint of history, that 1896 case and its reaffirmation in 1956 were correctly decided on the main question, whether a grant of full immunity against criminal prosecution supersedes the witness' right to refuse answer on grounds of self-incrimination.

Seventh, history lends no support to the 1972 opinion of the Court in *Kastigar v. United States* that anything less than full immunity satisfies the requirements of the Fifth. Justice Powell cited my book but still got the history wrong. You can lead a horse to water, but . . . The history of the matter, from the colonial period through Court opinions down to *Ullmann*, proves, as I indicated, that only a grant of full or transactional immunity abolishes the peril which justifies invocation of the Fifth.

Eighth, history also supports the decision made by the Court for the first time in 1955 that the right extends to legislative investigations. There were numerous instances in the colonial period of a witness claiming the right during an investigation conducted by a legislature. Colonial assemblies recognized the validity of such a claim; a few did not, but the Continental Congress did in 1778.

Ninth, history supports the 1897 rule of the Court that in criminal cases in the federal courts whenever a question arises whether a confession is incompetent because it is involuntary or coerced, the issue is controlled by the self-incrimination clause of the Fifth. Partly because of Wigmore's intimidating influence and partly because of the rule of *Twining* denying that the Fourteenth Amendment extended the Fifth to the states, the Court until 1964 held that the coercion of a confession by state or local authorities violated the principle of due process of law rather than the right against self-incrimination. Wigmore, the great master of evidence, claimed that the rule against coerced confessions and the right against self-incrimination had "no connection," the two being different in history, time of origin, principle, and practice. He was wrong on all counts.

Finally, history is ambiguous on the controversial issue of continuing interest, whether the right against self-incrimination extends to the police station. However, the right against self-incrimination began as a protest against incriminating interrogation prior to formal accusation. That is, the maxim *nemo tenetur seipsum prodere* originally meant that no one was obliged to supply the evidence which could be used to indict him. Thus, from the very inception of the right, a suspect could invoke it at the earliest stages of his interrogation. In its *Miranda* decision in 1966 the Supreme Court expanded the right beyond all precedent, yet not beyond its historical spirit and purpose.

Whether the Court ought to rely upon the wisdom and insights of the past when construing the right in question has not been my concern. The issue I raised is whether the Court has used the evidence of history knowledgeably and responsibly in its Fifth Amendment opinions. I conclude that it has not. Yet, without knowing it, by blunder or instinct the Court—until recently—has handed down opinions that have had a strong ally in history in keeping the Fifth "as broad as the mischief against which it seeks to guard."

The First Amendment:
Freedom of Speech

Donald Meiklejohn

THE THEME OF THIS DISCUSSION IS MR. JUSTICE BLACK'S emphasis on the public significance of First Amendment freedoms—their role as essential elements of American democracy. I do not mean to deny or to slight his devotion to individual values.[1] But I believe that in the many constitutional battles of his career, it was the public speech theme, articulated through the First Amendment, that provided the decisive thrust.

Mr. Justice Black conceived his constitutional duty in terms of keeping faith with the Founders. They had, as he understood them, a clear vision of the Bill of Rights as the heart of American democracy. Our Constitutional Faith bids us be true to their understandings and intentions. Of course, they lived long ago. But the Justice remarked in his James Madison Lecture:

> I cannot agree with those who think of the Bill of Rights as an 18th century straitjacket, unsuited for this age. It is old, but not all old things are bad. The evils it guards against are not only old, they are with us now, they exist today.[2]

As a Senator, Hugo Black was no enemy of new ideas and policies, but this did not qualify his devoted fidelity, on the

Supreme Court, to the permanent constitutional understandings that inform our common life.

Why should we, still, adhere to the Founders' intentions?
The Justice's answer makes explicit the relation between the
Bill of Rights and American democracy. The Bill of Rights is
not just a charter of individual immunities from government
interference. More fundamentally, as Federalist #84 argues, it
provides when taken with the Constitution as a whole the
political privileges which constitute us a political body, which
make us into a people who can decide our own character and
career. Indifference to the Founders is indifference to our-
selves. The heart of the Constitution is the process by which
our basic decisions are made; this is why no law may be passed
which abridges the essential elements in that process. The
Justice wrote, dissenting, in *Milk Wagon Drivers Union v.
Meadowmoor Dairies*, 312 U.S. 287, 301–02:

> Freedom to speak and write about public questions is as impor-
> tant to the life of our government as is the heart to the human
> body. In fact, this privilege is the heart of our government. If
> that heart be weakened, the result is debilitation; if it be stilled,
> the result is death.

In talking with Professor Cahn about the James Madison
Lecture, Mr. Justice Black observed:

> I confess not only that I think the [First] Amendment means
> what it says, but also that I may be slightly influenced by the
> fact that I do not think Congress *should* make any laws with
> respect to these subjects.[3]

With all deference, we may suggest that the distance is not
great between the true account of the Amendment's meaning
and the Justice's own opinion. For the Founders' intention and
his thinking are parts of that continuous whole which is the
American democratic career. The Founders are not just

eighteenth-century characters; they live in the Constitution of the America they established, as Mr. Justice Black lives and will live in his contribution to our self-government. Keeping faith with the Founders does not simply fulfill a contractual obligation; it affirms that part of us which endures as the vital impulse of our national community.

The First Amendment commits us to a certain procedure for making national decisions. It does not determine the content of those decisions—as to whether our governing should be centralized, or active in regulating the economy, or solicitous about the development of the arts and sciences. On those matters, policies will and should change. But what must not change is the mustering of our common powers of decision. Indeed, that prescription sets limits to policy, insofar as policy exercises a chilling or warming, a contracting or expansive influence on the forming of public opinion.

Why does the First Amendment provide a determinate, an absolute condition for policy? The answer is, for the same reason that the Constitution absolutely limits policy. We do not balance the Constitution against national security, or internal peace, or decency. Those ends are within the Constitution, not outside it. Likewise the First Amendment prescribes that we seek those ends through the public process of speech and counterspeech that is the essence of self-government. It is this view of the First Amendment, which I venture to call a public speech theory, that I shall try here to associate with the thinking of Mr. Justice Black.

The First Amendment is our charter of national citizenship, a citizenship which the Justice described as "beyond price."[4] To explain fully the Amendment's import for citizenship in our democracy would require attention to opinions on voting,[5] on representation,[6] on immigration and deportation,[7] on travel at home[8] and abroad;[9] and with these we shall have no time to deal. But they should be kept in mind as continuous with the freedom of speech, which is here our central concern.

The speech which Mr. Justice Black regarded as absolutely protected by the First Amendment was identified by contrast with expressions which subject other people to coercion.[10] When coercion occurs, we are in the realm of action, where others are affected whether they will or not. Speech works toward community of understanding and intention; in action we are actually or potentially in collision with others. In speech we enlarge others' freedom; in action we limit that freedom. Actions may call for regulation. But where expressions leave others free to accept or reject them, there is no justification for intervention by government.

Absolute protection for the free exchange of ideas is thus the rule. Restriction always must be justified by showing that expressions are so close to action that words are "used with all the effect of force."[11] Mr. Justice Black's theory of free expression may accordingly be explained in terms of proposals that have been advanced to limit free expression; we shall ask how far he believed that restrictions are justified by considerations:

(1) National security

(2) The reputations or feelings of other persons

(3) "Decency"

(4) The public peace, in the context of picketing, parades, and demonstrations

(5) The demands of special activities, such as government employment, legislatures, legal proceedings, and schools

(6) Privacy

(7) Finally, we shall consider briefly the bearing of the theory here advanced on the religion clauses of the First Amendment.

(1) Mr. Justice Black found little validity in proposals in the name of national security to restrict speech on public affairs. His response to the many legislative efforts to cripple the Communist Party in its alleged preparation to overthrow the American government followed two main lines of argument.

On the one hand, he contended, many of such efforts constituted bills of attainder, which are proscribed in the Constitution in terms as uncompromising as those of the First Amendment.[12] Prohibition of paying wages to alleged Communists in government employment,[13] or exclusion from labor union offices dealing with the National Labor Relations Board of persons failing to complete a non-Communist affidavit[14] was—as Mr. Justice Black thought—a way of attainting a group of persons without the due process required in ascription of guilt; we had returned, in effect to the eighteenth-century practice of declaring a corruption of political blood. A bill of attainder declared that a sector of the public did not qualify for participation in the process of self-government. Speech was restricted, not by its continuity with dangerous actions, but by the supposed bad company kept by the speaker.

In the second place, Mr. Justice Black found the national security attack on the protection of Communist political activity vitiated by the appeal to the tests of "clear and present danger"[15] and of balancing. He explained his view of the danger test in his conversation with Professor Edmond Cahn about the famous example offered by Mr. Justice Holmes, that "the most stringent protection of free speech would not justify shouting 'Fire' falsely in a crowded theater and causing a panic."[16] Such an expression can be restricted, Mr. Justice Black observed, not because of "what he hollered, but because he hollered,"[17] in a context where the result could be expected to be "panic"—a submissive and unreflective reaction. The content of the Communists' "shouting," the Justice noted,[18] is "mostly turgid, diffuse, abstruse, and just plain dull"; and "no juror is expected to plow his way through this jungle of verbiage." But the conduct of the Communist leaders involved no more than attending, and agreeing to attend, constitutionally protected meetings. In the name of the clear and present danger, said the Justice, men were being punished for their beliefs:

> [In essence] petitioners were tried upon the charge that they
> believe in and want to foist upon this country a different and to
> us a despicable form of authoritarian government in which
> voices criticizing the existing order are summarily silenced. I
> fear that the present type of prosecutions are more in line with
> the philosophy of authoritarian government than with that ex-
> pressed by the First Amendment.

Mr. Justice Black dissented with equal firmness from
balancing First Amendment protections against other values
such as national security. In *Barenblatt v. United States*, [19] dealing with a witness' refusal on First Amendment grounds to
answer questions put by the House Un-American Activities
Committee about his relationships with the Communist Party,
the Justice rejected the contention that Congress could abridge
speech and association if "this Court decides that the governmental interest is greater than an individual's interest in
exercising such freedom." There are, he acknowledged, situa-
tions in which expressions merge with actions—such as distri-
buting handbills on the streets, [20] or accosting others to ex-
pound a religious belief; [21] and keeping the streets clean, or
open to traffic, can be legitimately provided for even if there is
an indirect impact on freedom of expression.

> But we did not remotely suggest that a law directly aimed at
> curtailing speech and political persuasion could be saved by a
> balancing process. [22]

In addition, if balancing were to be admitted here, the Court
should weigh, not just the individual witness' right to silence,
but the interests of society in having

> people able to join organizations, advocate causes, and make
> "political mistakes" without later being subject to gov-
> ernmental penalties for having dared to think for themselves. [23]

And to the argument that the Government's right to preserve itself must be balanced against the First Amendment, the Justice responded:

> The First Amendment means to me that the only constitutional way our Government can preserve itself is to leave its people the fullest possible freedom to praise, criticize, or discuss, as they see fit, all governmental policies and to suggest, if they desire, that even its most fundamental policies should be changed.[24]

The Court should not, in the name of balancing and weighing, metaphorically hold in either hand, with eyes closed, competing gravities of such entities as individual freedom and public security. Such pretended measurement is deeply subjective and virtually certain to favor the supposed public need over the individual. The "weighing" which Mr. Justice Black did accept involved accommodating or reconciling to one another constitutional claims none of which could be ignored. It is possible to maintain full freedom of discussion without imperiling national security; it may be impossible to promote national security without fully free discussion.

In concluding his dissent in the Barenblatt case, Mr. Justice Black took note of the contention that the investigation which the Court upheld was after all only of Communists, and alleged Communists. He pointed out that many prominent Americans had objected on constitutional grounds to outlawing the Communist Party, and he recalled that in the non-Communist affidavit case ten years before the majority had disclaimed any effort to attaint the Communist Party and its members. Yet, he wrote:

> Today Communists, or suspected Communists, have been denied an opportunity to work as government employees, lawyers, doctors, teachers, pharmacists, veterinarians, subway conductors, industrial workers, and just about any other job... Nevertheless, this Court still sits![25]

In the 1960s Mr. Justice Black's objections to restrictions on the political expressions of Communists and other unpopular groups gained influence, though not ascendancy, in the Court. In a series of cases the recognition came to prevail that membership should be judged on an individual basis. Thus in the 1963 decision in *Gibson v. Florida Legislative Investigation Committee*,[26] the Court, per Mr. Justice Goldberg, ruled that the Miami branch of the NAACP need not disclose information which was demanded on the ground that some of its members were Communists. Mr. Justice Black, asserted:

> the constitutional right of association includes the privilege of any person to associate with Communists, or anti-Communists, Socialists, or anti-Socialists, or for that matter with people of all kinds of beliefs, popular or unpopular.[27]

In dissent, Mr. Justice Harlan contended that *Barenblatt* had established the propriety of investigating Communist influence in nonsubversive organizations.[28]

Two decisions near the end of Mr. Justice Black's term confirmed the strength of his achievement. A per curiam decision upset the conviction of a Ku Klux Klan leader for holding a meeting in an Ohio meadow;[29] Justices Black and Douglas, concurring separately, reiterated their beliefs that "the 'clear and present danger' doctrine should have no place in the interpretation of the First Amendment."[30] And Mr. Justice Black wrote the eloquent opinion in *New York Times v. United States* and *United States v. Washington Post*, refusing to sustain an injunction against their publishing the "Pentagon Papers"—the Defense Department's classified *History of United States Decision-Making Process on Vietnam Policy*. The opinion stated, in part:

> I believe that every moment's continuance of the injunction against these newspapers amounts to a flagrant, indefensible and continuing violation of the First Amendment . . . Now, for

the first time in the 182 years since the founding of the Republic, the Federal Courts are asked to hold that the First Amendment does not mean what it says, but rather means that the Government can halt the publication of current news of vital importance to the people of this country.

The press was to serve the governed, not the governors. The government's power to censure the press was abolished so that the press would remain forever free to censure the government. The press was protected so that it could bare the secrets of government and inform the people. Only a free and informed press can effectively expose deception in government. And paramount among the responsibilities of a free press is the duty to prevent any part of the government from deceiving the people and sending them off to foreign lands to die of foreign fevers and foreign shot and shell. In my view, far from deserving condemnation for their courageous reporting, The New York Times and The Washington Post and other newspapers should be commended for serving the purposes that the Founding Fathers saw so clearly.[31]

Separate concurrences were written by Justices Brennan, Douglas, Marshall, Stewart, and White. Of the three dissenters,[32] Mr. Chief Justice Burger wrote: "Only those who view the First Amendment as an absolute in all circumstances—a view I respect but reject—can find such a case as this to be simple or easy." Why not, he suggested, have the papers review with the government what can safely be published? Mr. Justice Harlan challenged the need for immediate decision. And Mr. Justice Blackmun declared "I cannot subscribe to a doctrine of unlimited absolutism for the First Amendment at the cost of downgrading other provisions" of the Constitution.

Mr. Justice Black's disagreement with his colleagues cannot fairly be described as that of "absolutism" versus "nonabsolutism." Restrictions of political expressions in the name of clear and present danger, or balancing, put into the hands of government officials power to decide who can, and who cannot, participate in the processes of self-government. Officials are given the authority to determine whether any particular opinion is worth hearing. Such a decision is as "absolute" as any interpretation of the First Amendment could be. And it contracts the basis for public decision, whereas Mr. Justice Black's view keeps that basis indefinitely open. The attack on Mr. Justice Black's "absolute" rests upon an absolute reliance on the wisdom of public officials.[33]

(2) Damage to the reputations or feelings of other persons is not, generally, a basis—on Mr. Justice Black's theory—for limiting the protections of the First Amendment. In *A Constitutional Faith* the Justice asserted: "I believe that the First Amendment compels the striking down of all libel laws."[34] He had concurred in Mr. Justice Murphy's doctrine that there are "fighting words"[35] which the First Amendment does not protect, but he dissented from application of this doctrine, in the Illinois Group Libel Law case,[36] in which the Court sustained the conviction of a pamphleteer for charging Negroes in Chicago with being "rapists, robbers, gun-carriers and drug-users." The Justice affirmed a very narrow interpretation of the fighting words doctrine:

> Every expansion of the law of criminal libel so as to punish discussion of matters of public concern means a corresponding invasion of the areas dedicated to free expression by the First Amendment.[37]

The words used were, however unpleasant, part of "arguments on questions of public interest and importance," and minority groups, hailing this decision, might well remember the ancient lament: "Another such victory, and I am undone!"[38]

In *New York Times v. Sullivan*[39] in 1964 and in *Garrison v. Louisiana*[40] eight months later, the Court unanimously invoked the First Amendment to strike down civil and criminal libel convictions based on criticisms of public officials. Mr. Justice

Brennan wrote the opinion in both cases, and in both he stressed the essential connection between free discussion and self-government. But in both cases he limited First Amendment protection to such expressions as are not "actually malicious,"[41] that is, deliberately false or made with reckless disregard for the truth. This restriction was rejected in *New York Times* by Justices Black, Douglas, and Goldberg, Black writing:

> I vote to reverse exclusively on the ground that the Times and the individual defendants had an absolute unconditional right to publish in the Times advertisement their criticisms of the Montgomery agencies and their officials.
>
> This Nation, I suspect, can live in peace without libel suits based on public discussions of public affairs and public officials. But I doubt that a country can live in freedom where its people can be made to suffer physically or financially for criticizing their government, its actions, or its officials. An unconditional right to say what one pleases about public affairs is what I consider to be the minimum guarantee of the First Amendment.[42]

In the *Garrison* case, concurring, he wrote that the test of "actual malice" revives "the old discredited English Star Chamber law of seditious criminal libel";[43] and he joined in the assertion by Mr. Justice Douglas that the Illinois Group Libel Law decision

> should be over-ruled as a misfit in our constitutional system and as out of line with the dictates of the First Amendment. [T]he only line drawn by the Constitution is between "speech" on the one hand and "conduct" or "overt acts" on the other.[44]

In the libel cases which followed, Mr. Justice Black, while rejecting the "actual malice" doctrine, generally agreed with the results reached by Mr. Justice Brennan. But in *Curtis*

Publishing Co. v. Butts[45] in 1967 Mr. Justice Black saw his
forebodings about the doctrine amply justified. In that case,
Mr. Justice Harlan, speaking also for Justices Clark, Fortas,
and Stewart, asserted that in the context of state libel legislation, publications may forfeit their protection when they are
"highly unreasonable," that is, "uttered without reasonable
care." Wally Butts, Georgia football coach, had sued the Curtis Publishing Company for an article in the *Saturday Evening
Post* which asserted that he had revealed his game plan to the
opposing coach. The Supreme Court ruled 5–4 in Butts's favor, Mr. Chief Justice Warren providing the decisive vote on
the ground that the *Post* was guilty under the *Times* "actual
malice" standard,[46] though not under Harlan's test, which the
Chief Justice described as "an unusual and uncertain formulation." Mr. Justice Brennan, in dissent,[47] faulted the charge to
the jury but conceded that the *Post* could be censured as "actually malicious." In the face of this variety Mr. Justice Black,
dissenting, wrote that the case

> illustrates, I think, the accuracy of my prior predictions that
> the New York Times constitutional rule concerning libel is
> wholly inadequate to save the press from being destroyed by
> libel judgments. . . . It strikes me that the Court is getting itself
> in the same quagmire in the field of libel in which it is now
> helplessly struggling in the field of obscenity.[48]

In 1970 the Court was asked to review the conviction for
libel of Ralph Ginzburg,[49] who had been sued by Senator
Goldwater for having published during the Presidential cam-
paign of 1964 an article offering evidence that Senator Goldwater was psychologically unfit for high office. The Court
declined to review. In dissenting from the denial, Mr. Justice
Black wrote:

> doubtless the jury was justified in this case in finding that
> the . . . articles on Senator Goldwater were prepared with a

reckless disregard for the truth. [Yet] High emotions and deep prejudices frequently pervade local communities where libel suits are tried. . . . Extravagant reckless statements and even claims that may not be true seem an inevitable part of the process by which the public informs itself.[50]

The actual malice test invites restriction whenever public discussion becomes serious. Talk will be "uninhibited, robust and wide-open"[51] when men are struggling to bring their fighting faiths to victory. One sees his opponent as hostile to the public good, and endeavors so to exhibit him in the public view. But damage done through speech and press calls for redress through the good sense of the public audience, not the discretion of public officials.[52]

Mr. Justice Black also insisted on First Amendment protections for speakers arousing hostility toward themselves or other persons.[53] He concurred in decisions upsetting convictions of Jehovah's Witnesses who proclaimed their faith in unfriendly neighborhoods[54] or rang doorbells in search of converts.[55] He concurred in reversing conviction of an unfrocked Catholic priest for delivering, in a Chicago hall surrounded by an angry mob, a speech spiced with epithets such as "slimy scum," "snakes," and "bed-bugs";[56] in dissent, Mr. Justice Jackson deplored the tendency to turn the Bill of Rights into a suicide pact. Mr. Justice Black also concurred in reversing the conviction[57] of a Baptist minister under a New York City statute requiring a license to hold religious meetings in public places; the minister, Kunz, had called the Pope "anti-Christ" and Jews "Christ-killers" who deserve to be "burnt in the incinerators." On the other hand, Mr. Justice Black concurred without comment in Mr. Chief Justice Hughes's opinion upholding the conviction for unlawful parading of a group of Jehovah's Witnesses;[58] the licensing law in that case, said the opinion, was precise and did not allow improper discretion to officials in judging the content of what the paraders said.

Later cases bring us into the cold war period. In *Feiner v. New York*[59] Mr. Justice Black dissented from upholding the conviction of a Syracuse University student who spoke at a street-corner criticizing the President and local officials. To the Chief Justice's contention that the State must have authority to prevent incitement to riot, Mr. Justice Black rejoined that it is customary on such occasions for people to "mutter, mill about, push, shove, or disagree, even violently, with the speaker."[60] The police, he argued, should have recognized their obligation to protect Feiner's constitutional right to speak, rather than arresting him: "he was entitled to know why he should cease doing a lawful act. Not once was he told." And in 1969 Mr. Justice Black joined three other Justices in a per curiam dismissal[61] of a conviction of a speaker who, on the Washington Monument grounds, had declared that, having received his draft notice, he was "not going" and that, "if they ever make me carry a rifle, the first man I want to get in my sights is LBJ. They are not going to get me to kill my black brothers." Although the District Court, per Judge Burger, had found him guilty of threatening the President's life, even if he did not intend to carry out the threat,[62] the Supreme Court per curiam opinion described the utterance as "political hyperbole." In Mr. Justice Black's theory, free speech protections extend to the raw material of group resentments, suspicions of authority, and willingness to defy officials. The Justice held to a serene faith in Americans' ability to listen to words they hate without in turn resorting to violent action.

Two cases involving so-called "symbolic speech" show the difficulty of distinguishing sharply, as Mr. Justice Black proposed, between speech and conduct. He concurred with the opinion of Mr. Chief Justice Warren confirming the conviction of a draftee who publicly burned his draft card on the statehouse steps in Boston.[63] He also took the position, in dissent, that First Amendment protection did not extend to burning an American flag on a New York City street by a Negro protesting the shooting of James Meredith in Mississippi.[64] The flag-burning was accompanied by the declaration, "If they did that to Meredith, we don't need an American flag." The Court's majority found the words the crucial factor and so ruled in favor of the flag-burner, but Mr. Justice Black argued that the flag-burning was the basis of the conviction. It was inconceivable he said that "anything in the Federal Constitution bars a State from making the deliberate burning of the American flag an offense." In these cases I have, I must confess, difficulty in accepting his conclusions. He reasons in each case, apparently, on the premise that conduct, rather than communication, is the matter at issue. But the conduct seems primarily aimed to communicate, noncoercively. And respect for the material embodiments of our public values did not appear decisive in the flag salute case in *West Virginia v. Barnette.*[66]

(3) Mr. Justice Black's attitude toward so-called "obscenity" may be described as "weary tolerance." He thought efforts to define obscenity doomed to failure; he also thought the subjects normally identified as obscene appropriate topics of discussion by a self-governing public. Although on his own account he did not always read or view the works on which the Court had to pass judgment,[67] there is no evidence that he believed other members of the Court would be the worse for reading or viewing them.[68] Nor did he, so far as I know, make explicit concessions to claims that juveniles should be shielded from pornography; he did concur in the remark of Mr. Justice Douglas that "most of the juvenile delinquents I know are over fifty."[69] What Mr. Justice Black did believe, earnestly, was that the people, not the government, should decide what is to be read and seen. Literature, art, drama, radio, television, all provide material about which the public is forever making up its mind. Conceding, in *A Constitutional Faith,*[70] that political speech—about elections, legislation, and administration—was

the primary concern of the First Amendment's Framers, he extended that concern to the wider area from which criteria for all political judgments must be drawn. Political importance is potentially as wide as the entire field of our common social experience.

The ruling test in this area was formulated in 1957 in the *Roth* case by Mr. Justice Brennan;[71] citing Mr. Justice Murphy's exclusion from First Amendment protections of the "lewd and the obscene,"[72] Mr. Justice Brennan declared a three-fold definition of obscenity—that it excite "prurient interest," that it offend contemporary community standards, and that it be "utterly lacking in redeeming social value." Mr. Justice Black joined with Mr. Justice Douglas in rejecting the *Roth* test on the ground that it called for punishment of thoughts as distinct from overt actions.[73]

In 1966 the Court considered cases involving the circulation of the novel *Fanny Hill* in Massachusetts,[74] the sale of allegedly dirty books in New York City,[75] and the sales publicity employed by Ralph Ginzburg in marketing his magazine *EROS*.[76] Mr. Justice Brennan and the Court majority declined to find *Fanny Hill* obscene under the *Roth* test, but they did sustain convictions of the bookseller and of Ginzburg, the latter for the "pandering character" of his sales pitch. In the two latter cases, Mr. Justice Black dissented. The vagueness of the definition of "obscenity," he said, left censorship to the discretion of public officials, and he thought the Supreme Court as unfitted as any other officials to play the censorial role:

> I believe the Federal Government is without any power whatever under the Constitution to put any type of burden on speech and expression of ideas of any kind. . . . For myself, I would follow the course which I believe is required by the First Amendment, that is, recognize that sex, at least as much as any other aspect of life, is so much a part of our society that its discussion should not be made a crime.[77]

We may note that after Mr. Justice Black left the Court, the *Roth* test was explicitly given up, the Court per Mr. Chief Justice Burger returning determination of obscenity to local jurisdictions[78] and Mr. Justice Brennan confessing[79] that the *Roth* test had not provided a satisfactory basis for decision. Mr. Justice Brennan wrote:

> I know of no satisfactory answer to the assertion of Mr. Justice Black "after the fourteen separate opinions handed down" in the trilogy of cases decided in 1966 that "no person, not even the most learned judge, much less a layman, is capable of knowing in advance of an ultimate decision in his particular case by this Court whether certain material comes within the area of 'obscenity'" *Ginzburg v. United States* 383 U.S. at 480-1 (dissenting opinion).[80]

We may imagine Mr. Justice Black smiling gently at his learned colleagues. But we need to ask whether his argument against censorship is only negative, or whether nonpolitical literature and art may on affirmative grounds be accorded First Amendment protection.

Such a positive answer is provided in the fuller text of his *Ginzburg* dissent:

> Sex is a fact of life. Its pervasive influence is felt throughout the world, and it cannot be ignored. Like all other facts of life, it can lead to difficulty and trouble and sorrow and pain. But while it may lead to abuses, and has in many instances, no words need be spoken in order for people to know that the subject is one pleasantly interwoven in all human activities and involves the very substance of the creation of life itself. It is a subject which people are bound to consider and discuss whatever laws are passed by any government to try to suppress it.[81]

Not only the unintelligibility of censorship but the positive importance of sex in our common experience dictate assurance of the protections of the First Amendment.[82]

(4) Mr. Justice Black's First Amendment theory as applied to group expressions presents greater complexity than has been apparent in the areas so far considered. When people parade, or demonstrate, or picket, the element of coercion—potential or actual—normally increases. Yet at the same time, the importance of the public communication involved may also increase. Mr. Justice Black was sensitive to both sides of the situation, and his opinions constitute a continuing effort to do justice to both.[83] Although I shall offer reservations about some of his conclusions, I shall do so in the spirit of a perplexed fellow-traveler in an uncertain field.

We have broadly two sets of cases to consider—the labor disputes, mainly in the 1940s and 1950s, and the civil rights demonstrations of the 1960s. In 1939 Mr. Justice Black concurred in the opinion of Mr. Justice Roberts upholding the right of the CIO and other groups to meet in Jersey City despite the prohibitions of Mayor Frank ("I am the Law") Hague.[84] The Roberts opinion affirmed the basic premise of a "First Amendment society"—that is, that citizens are protected in discussing public affairs, anywhere, anytime, anyhow, *except* as appropriate reasons exist to qualify such protection

> wherever the title of streets and parks may rest, they have immemorially been held in trust for the public and, time out of mind, have been used for the purposes of assembly, communicating thoughts between citizens, and discussing public questions.[85]

The streets are the poor people's meeting-halls, as leaflets are the poor man's printing press.

The theme of the public importance of canvassing the issues of the time, in the context of picketing in a company town, was reiterated a year later by Mr. Justice Murphy, with Mr. Justice Black again concurring.[86] On the other hand, in commenting in *A Constitutional Faith* in 1969 on this opinion, Mr. Justice Black characterized the decision as based rather upon the vice of over-breadth in the statute than on a directly First Amendment consideration.[87] The more precise statement of his own position, he said, had been presented in 1949 in which he had excluded from First Amendment protections those expressions which are "mixed with conduct"; for this reason he had upheld an injunction against peaceful picketing which was employed in conflict with a state policy regulating labor relations.[88] And yet again, throughout the 1940s and 1950s, and in a notable concurring opinion in 1964,[89] he had indicated that in picketing cases the public's interest in being informed must always be accorded a high priority.

It is the relation between the "speech" and the "conduct" elements in picketing and demonstrating that makes trouble for theory as well as for practical decision. Sometimes, the Justice seemed to say that while "pure speech," wholly divorced from conduct, is fully protected, "impure speech," which is inextricably mixed with conduct, enjoys no protection at all. But there are impurities in all communication—it all involves somebody being somewhere, sometime, and speaking in a certain way. The crucial question is whether the impurity reaches the level of staining the human interchange with genuine coercion of other people. Picket lines and parades may coerce, but they may simply communicate. This is explicitly acknowledged in many of Mr. Justice Black's opinions, and yet his more general statements seem to relegate the speech considerations in picketing and demonstrations to a definitely subordinate role. There is not, as there was in the leafletting cases earlier discussed, a determination to discover reconciliation between First Amendment purposes and other needs.

The same problems appear in the principal civil rights cases in the 1960s—the assembly of 2,000 black college students across the street from the Baton Rouge courthouse, protesting the arrest on charges of illegal picketing of fellow students the day before,[90] a quiet sit-in by five black youths in a Louisiana branch library,[91] a civil rights demonstration on the grounds of the South Carolina statehouse,[92] a similar demonstration on the premises of a Florida jail,[93] the Good Friday march in 1963 in Birmingham of black demonstrators associated with Martin Luther King, Jr.,[94] a protest march led by Dick Gregory in Chicago in criticism of Chicago school segregation,[95] a restaurant sit-in in Maryland.[96] A case involving picketing in a privately owned shopping plaza evoked the same principles of decision as those which just preceded it.[97] In all these cases Mr. Justice Black, while insisting that regulations must be clearly and specifically drawn, still contended that the demonstrators could not claim the unqualified protection of the First Amendment. The first question to be decided, he appeared to say, was whether they had a right to be where they were, at the given time. Accordingly, he maintained that the demonstrators in Baton Rouge could not claim protection, since they were picketing the courthouse,[98] that the library protesters could not upset the reading-room's tranquillity to conduct their sit-in,[99] that demonstrators on the jail grounds properly could be arrested for trespassing.[100] And thus he insisted that private restaurants[101] and shopping plazas[102] are not required to provide a platform for protesters against the segregated or antiunion character of the private firm. He did concur in judgments upsetting the convictions of the South Carolina and Chicago marchers, since in those cases the regulations were, as he thought, impermissibly broad[103] or left too much discretion to the policeman on the beat.[104]

My difficulty with his reasoning as it went against the demonstrators is that the First Amendment considerations seem to have virtually disappeared. Granted that a courthouse must not be closely invested by large groups of people, cannot a demonstration appropriately remote claim protection even if it intimates resentment of arrests made the day before? Granted that a library must preserve quiet, cannot a silent sit-in to protest well-known segregation be so conducted as not to upset the library routine? Can crowds on jail grounds, or sit-ins or pickets on private premises never so manage their behavior as to be justified in making their case public despite the opposition of officials or private owners? These are not easy questions in practice, and one's answer will depend upon factors of distance, crowd attitudes, availability of the forces of law and order, as these are found in the various cases. But surely the need for the public to know, and for the participants to make their case to the public, must be accorded as much attention as possible; it does not simply deserve consideration after the other "proprieties" have received their due.

Mr. Justice Black sometimes spoke of "weighing" the circumstances when conduct, as distinct from speech, was involved, but "accommodation" or "reconciliation" seems a more appropriate conception. If courthouses, libraries, state legislatures, jails, and private establishments must be unhindered in the transaction of their regular business, still their approaches, if not too closely invested, seem especially appropriate for demonstrations. Good Friday in 1963 in Birmingham surely was peculiarly suitable for a march protesting segregation; I find it difficult to follow the argument, in which Mr. Justice Black concurred, that an injunction against the march should have been challenged instead of disobeyed.[105] If one can claim First Amendment protection only when he is at the right place and time and speaking in the right way, still the rightness must be determined in part by reference to the First Amendment, that is, by determining what the available forms of expression are there, and then.

The wave of student protests in our schools and colleges in the late 1960s and early 1970s was marked by persistent absences from classes—not, in itself, unusual—but also by demonstrations *in* classrooms to take up topics not on the official calendar. Between indifference and obstreperous intrusions there sometimes developed intermediate expressions, like that in an Iowa high school in which a few students defied an official ban against wearing black armbands on the school premises.[106] The ban reflected the school authorities' concern that—in light of the recent death of a graduate of the school in Vietnam—symbolic protests against the war policy might upset the school's regular business. The armband-wearing students having been duly suspended and sent home, their parents sought an injunction against the ban, were unsuccessful in District Court, but won their case in the Supreme Court, Mr. Justice Fortas writing that the armband wearing was a protected form of public communication. Mr. Justice Black could not agree. He saw the armbands as a source of distraction and effectively a takeover of the school by the children:

> If pupils can flout school officials, the judiciary will be fostering a new revolutionary era of permissiveness. . . . The original idea of school, which I do not believe is yet abandoned or out of date, was that children had not yet reached the point of experience and wisdom which enabled them to teach all of their elders . . . This case . . . wholly without constitutional reason, in my judgment, subjects all the public schools in the country to the whims and caprices of their loudest-mouthed but maybe not their brightest students. I, for one, am not fully persuaded that schools' pupils are wise enough, even with this Court's expert help from Washington, to run the 23,300 public school systems in our fifty states.[107]

Few academic persons would challenge this as a statement of general principle. But the record does not show any serious disruption of school routines; there was some controversial comment by other students, and a protracted argument between a teacher and one of the armband wearers in a mathematics class. The imposition of the ban appears to reflect both insecurity on the part of the school officials and a partiality toward the "patriotic" side of the argument over the Vietnam War. The schools, it would seem, should be able to accommodate and contain the extension of a burning public debate within the school premises, as Mr. Justice Fortas said,

> The unmistakable holding of this Court for almost fifty years has been that students and teachers take with them into the school house gate constitutional rights to freedom of speech and expression.[108]

Unless regular school procedures were actively interrupted, one would think that a gesture of symbolic mourning deserved protection quite as much as would the wearing of an armband for the death of a particular relative or friend.

(5) The issues we have considered in relation to demonstrations have already suggested that special problems attend the protections to be accorded speech in special areas. The great single town meeting of public discussion which the Supreme Court moderates is complemented by many special meetings where special functions are performed in the public interest. Of these we shall consider government employment generally, legislatures, legal proceedings, and schools. In these, while acknowledging the propriety of special restrictions, Mr. Justice Black affirmed the widest possible application of First Amendment principles.

Government Employment. In 1947 the Supreme Court upheld the Hatch Act, which made unlawful any "active part in political management or political campaigns" by governmental employees.[109] Mr. Justice Black, dissenting, noted that three million Federal and thousands of state employees were involved. It does no good to say that they could still express opinions, he wrote,

> Real popular government means that "men may speak as they think on matters vital to them and that falsehoods may be exposed through the processes of education and discussion"

(quoted from *Thornhill v. Alabama* 310 U.S. 88, 95). . . . There
is nothing about federal and state employees as a class which
justifies depriving them or society of the benefits of their participation in public affairs. . . . Our political system rests on
rule by all the people.[110]

Abuses in the form of coercion could, he thought, be punished
separately.

Legislatures. Mr. Justice Black concurred in the Court's reversal of the expulsion from the Georgia State Legislature of
Julian Bond who,[111] soon after his election, publicly endorsed
an attack by the Student Non-Violent Coordinating Committee against American Vietnam policy and also affirmed his
admiration for those brave enough to burn their draft cards.
The opinion, by the Chief Justice, declared for a unanimous
Court that Bond had not directly incited violation of the Selective Service Act and that Georgia's attempt to impose a special
loyalty standard contravened the principle that legislators be
given the widest possible latitude to express their views on
matters of policy. They must be committed, like other citizens, to "robust, uninhibited and wide-open discussion."

Legal Proceedings. Issues involving demonstrations near courthouses and jails have just been considered. Another problem
concerns the freedom to comment on pending or current court
proceedings; early in his term Mr. Justice Black wrote for a
five-man majority overturning contempt convictions of labor
leader Harry Bridges and the *Los Angeles Times* for comments
on the trial, and petitions for probation, of certain union officials.[112] The Justice wrote that the Bridges telegram which
called the conviction "outrageous" and the *Times* editorial
which "did no more than threaten future adverse criticism"
could not be regarded as offering a clear and present danger to
the judicial process.

The Court also has had to adjudicate controversies about
the qualifications of candidates for admission to the bar. In the

1940s and 1950s committees of character and fitness exhibited special sensitivity to problems of subversiveness or lack of fidelity to legal canons. Mr. Justice Black's opposition to political tests was persistent and eloquent. Dissenting in 1945 from Illinois' refusal to admit to the bar an applicant who conscientiously objected to military service, the Justice wrote

> A state cannot bar a well-qualified man from a "semi-public" position... solely because he entertains a religious belief which might prompt him at some time in the future to violate a law which has not been and may never be enacted.[113]

Twelve years later the Justice wrote for a six-man majority holding that an applicant might not be excluded from the bar because he had been affiliated with the Communist Party fifteen years earlier.[114] In the same session, however, he was again in a four-man minority in respect of the denial of admission to an applicant who refused to answer questions about membership in the Communist Party. The Justice wrote

> The interest in free association at stake here is not merely the personal interest in being free of burdens that may be imposed upon him for his past beliefs and associations. It is the interest of all the people in having a society in which no one is intimidated with respect to his beliefs or associations. It seems plain to me that the inevitable effect of the majority's decision is to condone a practice that will have a substantial deterrent effect upon the associations entered into by any one who may want to become a lawyer in California.[115]

Again on the same day, and speaking for the same minority, the Justice condemned the exclusion[116] from the Illinois bar of a candidate whose refusals to answer questions about connections with the Communist Party were, as Mr. Justice Black read the record, not shown to be associated with any link to the Party but were rather indications of courage and dedication to the Declaration of Independence.

Two cases early in 1971 brought the Court more nearly into agreement with Mr. Justice Black. In bar admission cases in Arizona[117] and Ohio[118] a majority of five, speaking through Mr. Justice Stewart, held that persons could not be excluded from the bar because of their political beliefs; the Court rejected the contention that candidates might be asked about their political beliefs with a view to determining their adherence to established procedures of justice. Mr. Justice Black, concurring, wrote:

> The foregoing cases and others contain thousands of pages of confusing formulas, refined reasonings and puzzling holdings, that touch on the same suspicions and fears about citizenship and loyalty. However, we have concluded that the best way to handle this case is to narrate its simple facts and then relate them to the 45 words that make up the First Amendment.[119]

On the other hand, Mr. Justice Black and his liberal colleagues failed to win Mr. Justice Stewart's vote in a New York case in which a law students group sought an injunction against the asking of questions about membership in organizations advocating overthrow of government by force and violence.[120] In dissent, Mr. Justice Black once again condemned the view that lawyers should be subject to requirements different from those applied to legislators or the general public; the First Amendment is for all citizens, he wrote, and a democratic society needs critical and independent lawyers.

The pursuit of justice through the law is at once general in its public importance and special in its demands for expertise and commitment. Lawyers must of course be dedicated to the canons through which the law provides its special service to the public. But as Mr. Justice Black teaches us, those very specialized proceedings of statement and counter-statement, by which individuals are accorded justice among themselves and with society, require the widest variety and the most energetic expression of differing perspectives, within the order of the Court. If lawyers must be especially well-behaved, they must also be especially independent.

Education. Our schools and colleges have been throughout the past forty years under pressures to promote particular conceptions of national well-being and security. Mr. Justice Black steadily resisted such pressures even though he acknowledged the problems arising from the pupils' immaturity. Teachers and students must be free, he contended, to follow the truth wherever it leads, and the only admissible bar to the full participation of teachers and students in the educational process is thus incompetence or actual obstruction of that process.

In 1943 Mr. Justice Black, together with Justices Douglas and Murphy, reversed the stand they had taken three years earlier in upholding a required flag salute in public schools.[121] Approval in the first case, Justices Black and Douglas said, reflected their reluctance to interfere with State regulation; but "long reflection" had convinced them that "a failure, because of religious scruples, to assume a particular physical position and to repeat the words of a patriotic formula" could not be said to create "a grave danger to the nation."[122]

> Neither our domestic tranquillity in peace nor our martial effort in war depend on compelling little children to participate in a ceremony which ends in nothing for them but a fear of spiritual condemnation.

A similar reversal in the Court's position, though not in that of Mr. Justice Black, involved New York State's Feinberg Law of 1949 which made membership in an organization teaching overthrow of government by force and violence—or the individual advocacy thereof—prima facie grounds for dis-

qualification from State employment. The Supreme Court in
1952 upheld the law,[123] Mr. Justice Minton declaring it appropriate as applied to teachers; "from time immemorial," he
wrote, "one's reputation has been determined in part by the
company he keeps" and teachers work with impressionable
minds. Dissenting for himself and Mr. Justice Douglas, Mr.
Justice Black wrote:

> public officials cannot be constitutionally vested with power to
> select the ideas people can think about, censor the public views
> they can express, or choose the persons or groups people can
> associate with. Public officials with such powers are not public
> servants; they are public masters.[124]

The Feinberg Law was effectively nullified in 1967.[125] Mr.
Justice Brennan, for the five-man majority that included Mr.
Justice Black, declared that the law's provisions regarding
seditious words or acts were so vague as to improperly restrict
First Amendment freedoms. Knowing membership in an organization, per se, was not ground for exclusion from State
employment; specific intent of further unlawful aims must be
shown. In dissent, Mr. Justice Clark protested the majority's
"blunderbuss" approach and insisted, in conclusion

> The issue here is a very narrow one... May the State pro-
> vide that one who, after a hearing with full judicial review, is
> found to have wilfully and deliberately advocated, advised, or
> taught that our Government should be overthrown by force
> and violent means, ... is prima facie to be excluded from teach-
> ing in its University? My answer, in keeping with all our cases
> until today, is Yes![126]

Can Mr. Justice Black's stand in these school cases be recon-
ciled with his dissent, above noted, in the Iowa school
armband case? I have difficulty, I confess, in distinguishing
between excluding alleged subversives from New York

schools and excluding antiwar mourning symbols from Iowa schools. The Justice's ground for distinction, I think, lay in the Iowa children's direct defiance of a regulation designed to prevent disorder in the school. The school authorities evidently believed that the students, and probably their parents, were trying to take over the school to register their protest, and this doubtless contributed to Mr. Justice Black's belief that the right order of education was being upset. I cannot believe, however, that he would have insisted upon a wholly uncritical attitude of students toward their teachers or other officials.

Special Areas and the Public. With respect to each of the areas we have considered it seems clear that Mr. Justice Black's primary concern was with the public mission to be served; though this did not mean that individual interests of government employees, or legislators, or lawyers, or teachers and students, were not to be considered. As one speaks of the public mission involved, however, it is clear that the First Amendment must be respected. Government offices, legislatures, courts, schools, are not required just to run smoothly. Equally, they must be faithful to the society they serve both in reflecting the opinions of the people from whom their members come and in offering to all, judged only in terms of their competence, a chance to participate. The doctrine must be rejected that such participation is a "privilege" and "not a right," to be allowed as officials may decide. The claim to participate is in principle like the claim to speak in public—a claim recognized for everyone except on grounds that are impartially and clearly defined in terms of the particular public objective involved.

(6) If the speech that enjoys First Amendment protection is that which deals with public matters, is there—in Mr. Justice Black's theory—a realm of private affairs which may not be discussed with the same constitutional protection? In the special areas we have just considered we have dealt with certain

recognized "privacies"—activities officially designated by the community to fulfill specified public purposes. Now we ask whether we, as individuals, also enjoy such special status as to limit other people's discussion about us. Does "privacy" impose limits on the protections of the First Amendment?

Mr. Justice Black's answer was broadly negative. He set forth his view of the constitutional status of privacy in dissenting from the decision,[127] in 1965, striking down Connecticut's anti-contraception law. He said that personally he disapproved of the law as public policy, but he condemned the appeal to "natural law" which he noted in the Court's opinion; he rejected also appeal to a "collective moral sense" or a "sense of fairness and justice" as a basis for decision. The Constitution should be taken to mean what it says, he declared, and here the relevant text is the Fourth Amendment's prohibition of unreasonable searches and seizures:

> I get nowhere in this case by talk about a constitutional "right of privacy" as an emanation from one or more constitutional provisions. . . . I like my privacy as well as the next one, but I am nevertheless compelled to admit that the government has a right to invade it unless prohibited by some specific constitutional provision.[128]

The depth of the disagreement between Mr. Justice Black and some of his colleagues on the privacy issue was revealed in *Time v. Hill*[129] in which a suit for invasion of privacy was brought against *Life* magazine for publishing a story about a Broadway play partly based on the nineteen-hour imprisonment of Hill's family by three escaped convicts. In part the disagreements in the Court involved the actual malice test considered above. But there also appeared divergent opinions about the status and identification of privacy. Mr. Justice Black, concurring in the decision rejecting Hill's petition, wrote:

If judges have, however, by their own fiat today created a right of privacy equal to or superior to the right of a free press that the Constitution created, then tomorrow and the next day and the next, judges can create more rights that balance away other cherished Bill of Rights freedoms. If there is one thing that could strongly indicate that the Founders were wrong in reposing so much trust in a free press, I would suggest that it would be for the press itself not to wake up to the grave danger to its freedom, inherent in this "weighing" process. *LIFE*'s conduct here was at most a mere understandable and incidental error of fact in reporting a newsworthy event. One does not have to be a prophet to foresee that judgments like the one we reverse can frighten and punish the press so much that publishers will cease trying to report news in a lively and readable fashion so long as there is—and there always will be—doubt as to the complete accuracy of the newsworthy facts.[130]

Identification of the Broadway play as a "newsworthy event" seemed to him to require no special argument. But a strenuous dissent by Mr. Justice Fortas,[131] joined by the Chief Justice and Mr. Justice Clark, protested that a distinct right of privacy is now widely recognized, that such a right had been described by Mr. Justice Brandeis as "the most comprehensive of rights and the right most valued by civilized man[132] and that the *Life* article "irresponsibly and injuriously invades the privacy of a private family for no purpose except dramatic interest and commercial appeal."[133] The press here was being immunized, argued the dissent, "in areas far beyond the needs of news, comment on public persons and events, discussion of public issues and the like."

In his concurring opinion in *New York Times v. Sullivan*, Mr. Justice Goldberg had suggested[134] that the First Amendment does not protect libels on people's private lives. It is plausible to argue that such a stipulation is practically meaningless—that, as Zechariah Chafee once remarked,[135] not law but the conscience of the press and people's good sense alone can pre-

vent intrusions into matters of no public interest. I do not find
in Mr. Justice Black's writing a definitive statement on this
issue. He did insist on full constitutional protection for such
"privacy" as was required by explicit Constitutional provisions—for the right to refuse to answer questions about
one's political beliefs[136] from Congressional committees or bar
admission committees.[137] He affirmed the rights of persons to
enjoy "domestic tranquillity" for repose and refreshment of
their capacity to participate in public life.[138] But beyond this I
understand him to say "The Constitution defines the conditions of our public being, and with respect to that we must live
by what the Constitution says; we have our moral convictions,
and our likes and dislikes, but these are not to be confused
with constitutional principles."

Thus so far as the relation between speech and privacy is
concerned, it appears that what is spoken or published is—
literally—public. What an individual keeps entirely to himself
is indubitably private; this was the Court's finding about Stanley's private pornographic films.[139] But what is communicated
to others in sound or print enters that public domain where
common understandings are formed and common actions gen-
erated. There are sounds and gestures—"fighting words," as
strictly defined, and the threats of aggressive demonstrators—which express only personal attitudes. But normally
words and publications carry with them public significance.

(7) As we conclude this study of the public reference in Mr.
Justice Black's First Amendment theory, we need to consider
briefly the bearing of that reference on the clauses relating to
religion. In answering Professor Cahn's questions about the
Bill of Rights, the Justice acknowledged[140] his belief that the
Framers' basic purpose in the First Amendment was to protect
political speech. He then added, "that, plus the fact that they
wanted to protect religious speech. Those were the two things
that they had in mind." At a later point in the interview,[141] he
said that the freedom of opinion is especially important "in the

field of religion, because a man's religion is between himself and his Creator, not between himself and his Government." Shall we infer, then, that in Mr. Justice Black's thinking the First Amendment has two independent lines of thought—the political, in which our public concerns are defined and protected, and the religious, in which through the nonestablishment and free exercise provisions, our private interests are protected from public interference?

There is no doubt that such a separation, illustrated in the metaphor of the Wall,[142] played an important part in his theory. No theme recurs more often in his opinions on religion than the disaster attendant upon attempts by religious sects or government to coerce the consciences of men;[143] no hero seems more appealing than John Lilburne,[144] affirming his convictions in the face of cruel and persistent persecution. The religion clauses surely do express the determination to prevent a terrible form of man's inhumanity to man. And in the opinion outlawing prayers in public schools Mr. Justice Black asserted that the "first and most immediate purpose of the Establishment clause rested on the belief that a union of government and religion tends to destroy government and to degrade religion."[145]

Yet a wholly negative doctrine of separation seems incomplete. For one thing, freedom of expression surely is continuous as it moves from political topics to religion. And there appear to be, further, areas in which more specific mutual support is consistent with the First Amendment. Such an area is indicated, I believe, in Mr. Justice Black's 1970 opinion on conscientious objection.[146]

Elliott Welsh was convicted of refusing to submit to induction into the Armed Forces and was sentenced to three years in prison. He had petitioned for the status of conscientious objector on the ground that he was conscientiously opposed to participation in war in any form. He had been brought up in a religious home and had attended a church—a nonpacifist church—in his childhood. In his original application for conscientious objector status, he did not attribute his opposition to combatant service to religious training and belief, nor did he affirm belief in a Supreme Being. His belief, as Mr. Justice Black noted "could not be said to come from a 'still small voice of conscience'; rather . . . that voice was so loud and insistent that he preferred to go to jail rather than serve in the Armed Forces."[147] There was never, the Justice said, "any question about the sincerity and depth of Welsh's convictions as a conscientious objector,"[148] and the Justice noted that Welsh had revised his petition to say that his beliefs were "certainly religious in the ethical sense of the word."[149] Mr. Justice Black's opinion, acknowledging that Congress had excluded as a basis for valid conscientious objector status beliefs that are "essentially political, sociological or philosophical . . . or a merely personal moral code,"[150] upheld the validity of Welsh's appeal, stating that the law "exempts from military service all those whose consciences, spurred by deeply held moral, ethical or religious beliefs, would give them no rest or peace if they allowed themselves to become part of an instrument of war."[151]

As I read this opinion, the Justice found Welsh qualified for objector status on the publicly acceptable ground that he was religiously pacifist. He was not just privately opposed to participating in the war, from fear or from political disagreement with the war policy. Rather, he was opposed to the public policy of settling disputes by destroying human life. He was on public ground in terms both of the public verifiability of his sincerity and its import for American policy-making.

Was the decision in Welsh, as Mr. Justice Harlan suggested,[152] in fact an establishment of religion—was Welsh accorded a privilege unavailable to a nonreligious pacifist? Here one must distinguish, I think, between sectarian religions, which are the object of the nonestablishment clause, and that wider nonsectarian religion, "of humanity" if you will, which Mr. Justice Black thought entitled Welsh to exemption. I am uncertain what the Justice would have said about this argument, but it seems to me that his reasoning in this case may be said to concern not the religions which divide men but that humane and universal religion which unites them. Religion, in conduct as well as belief, may be established insofar as its free exercise is congruent with the regime of rational persuasion in distinction from force. Welsh may be required to participate in a national undertaking in noncombatant ways, for these are appropriate to the kind of society to which his religion is committed.[153]

On the only occasion when I have been able to attend a session of the Supreme Court, I saw sitting side by side Mr. Justice Frankfurter—animated, restless, whispering—and Mr. Justice Murphy—rather stiff and often apparently disinterested except when the Bill of Rights was mentioned—and Mr. Justice Black—sitting between them with persistent and alert attention to the lawyers but also a relaxed ease in the company of his colleagues. No one would prescribe that the Supreme Court should so associate a Jewish member and a Catholic and a Southern Baptist, and yet surely it was fitting that the common elements of their different religions should inform their interpretations of our common political creed.

At the end of his James Madison Lecture in 1960 Mr. Justice Black said:

> Since the earliest days the philosophers have dreamed of a country where the mind and spirit of man should be free; where there would be no limits to inquiry; where men would be free to explore the unknown and to challenge the most deeply rooted beliefs and principles. Our First Amendment was a bold effort to adopt this principle—to establish a country with no legal restrictions of any kind upon the subjects men could investigate, discuss and deny. The Framers knew,

perhaps better than we do today, the risks they were taking. They knew that free speech might be the friend of change and revolution. But they also knew that it always is the deadliest enemy of tyranny. With this knowledge they still believed that the ultimate happiness and security of a nation lies in its ability to explore, to change, to grow and ceaselessly to adapt itself to new knowledge born of inquiry free from any governmental control over the mind and spirit of man. Loyalty comes from love of a good government, not fear of a bad one.[154]

The justice did not falter in his faith, at once political and religious, in men's ability to live together in freedom and mutual respect. As the Chief Justice so well said,[155] in the memorial meeting in Washington,

He believed in the people.

NOTES

1. In introducing his *A Constitutional Faith* (the James S. Carpentier Lectures in 1969 at Columbia University), Mr. Justice Black spoke of the Constitution as our unique contribution to securing a society in which individual liberty is secure against governmental oppression.

2. 35 *New York University Law Review* 879–80 (1960).

3. 37 *New York University Law Review* 549, 554 (1962).

4. Dissenting, in *Johnson v. Eisentrager*, 339 U.S. 763, 791: "Not only is U.S. citizenship a 'high privilege'—it is a priceless treasure. For that citizenship is enriched beyond price by our goal of equal justice under law."

5. In *William v. Rhodes* 89 S. Ct. 5, 10, 21 (1968) Mr. Justice Black wrote: "In the present situation the state laws place burdens on two different, though overlapping kinds of rights—the right of individuals to associate for the advancement of political beliefs and the right of qualified voters, regardless of their political persuasion, to cast their votes effectively. Both of these rights, of course, rank among our most precious freedoms. We have repeatedly held that freedom of association is protected by the First Amendment. Similarly, we have said of the right to vote: No right is more precious in a free country than that of having a voice in the election of those who made the laws under which, as good citizens, we must live. Other laws,

even the most basic, are illusory if the right to vote is undermind" (the Justice was writing in support of the claim to a place on the Ohio ballot of George Wallace and the Socialist Labor Party).

6. In *Wesberry v. Sanders* 84 S. Ct. 526 (1964), 376 U.S. 3, Mr. Justice Black asserted that Article I, "means that as nearly as is practicable one man's vote in congressional elections is to be worth as much as any other"—this is what "elected by the people means"—"No right is more precious." He further quoted Madison in *Federalist* #57:

> Who are to be the electors of the Federal Representatives? Not the rich, more than the poor; not the learned, more than the ignorant; not the haughty heirs of distinguished names, more than the humble sons of obscure and unpropitious fortune. The electors are to be the great body of the people of the United States.

7. Cf. *Bridges v. Wixon* 326 U.S. 135 (1946), *Ludecke v. Watkins* 335 U.S. 160 (1948) *United States v. Shaughnessy* 338 U.S. 521, *Harisiades v. Shaughnessy* 342 U.S. 580, *Carlson v. Landon* 342 U.S. 524, *United States v. Spector* 343 U.S. 169 (in this immigration case the Justice, dissenting, said "the present statute... entangles aliens in a snare of vagueness from which few can escape"—at 174), *Shaughnessy v. United States* 345 U.S. 206, *International Longshoremen and Warehousemen's Union v. Boyd* 347 U.S. 222, *Galvan v. Press* 347 U.S. 522. In these cases Mr. Justice Black, recurrently in dissent, spoke out against deportations based, as he believed, on political considerations and frequently lacking in full due process of law. In *Shaughnessy v. Pedreiro* 349 U.S. 48 he wrote the opinion affirming the need for judicial review of a deportation order; but in *Shaughnessy v. United States ex rel Accardi* 349 U.S. 280 (1954) he was in dissent from the Court's position that the Attorney-General had not prejudiced deportation proceedings by referring to the prospective deportee as a "racketeer." See also *Jay v. Boyd* 351 U.S. 345, *Rowoldt v. Perfetto* 355 U.S. 115, *Bonetti v. Rogers* 356 U.S. 691, *Niukkanen v. Alexander* 362 U.S. 391.

8. Cf. his concurrence in *Aptheker v. Secretary of State* 378 U.S. 500: the Subversive Activities Control Act, under which it was proposed to deny a passport to a Communist Party official, was, he wrote a bill of attainder; "The best way to promote the internal security of our people is to protect their First Amendment freedoms." At 518 see also *Kent v. Dulles* 357 U.S. 116, *Dayton v. Dulles* 357 U.S. 144, *Zemel v. Rusk* 381 U.S. 1.

9. *People of State of New York v. O'Neill* (dissent) 359 U.S. 1: "Whatever may be the source of this right of free movement—the right to go to any

State or stay home as one chooses—it is an incident of national citizenship
and occupies a high place in our constitutional values" at 14. Cf. *Edwards v.
California* 314 U.S. 160.

   10. *A Constitutional Faith*, p. 53.

   11. *Schenck v. United States* 249 U.S. 47 (1919), 52.

   12. Article I, section 9: No bill of Attainder . . . shall be passed; section 10:
No State shall pass any Bill of Attainder.

   13. *United States v. Lovett* 328 U.S. 303 (1946).

   14. *American Communications Association v. Douds* 339 U.S. 382 (1950). Mr.
Chief Justice Vinson distinguished the 9th provision of the Taft-Hartley
Act from a bill of attainder on the thesis that bills of attainder are retrospect-
ive, and that the provision did not restrict Communists' political activities
and affected only a few people; the Chief Justice's opinion also adumbrated
the revision of the danger test into the "grave and probable" form it assumed
in the Dennis case.

   15. Mr. Justice Black employed the language of the danger test in opinions
during the early years of his service on the Court, notably in *Bridges v.
California* 314 U.S. 252 (1941), but it seems clear that he interpreted it in the
strict sense defined in Mr. Justice Brandeis' concurring opinion in *Whitney v.
California* 274 U.S. 357, 376-77. In the World War II case most similar to
Schenck—Hartzell v. United States 322 U.S. 680—Mr. Justice Black concurred in reversing the conviction for conspiracy to violate the Espionage
Act of the author of anonymous letters to officers and soldiers attacking
United States war policy and expressing anti-semitic and anti-yellow races
sentiments. Mr. Justice Black formulated his objection to the danger test
expressly in *Dennis v. United States* (dissent) 341 U.S. 494 (1951), at 579-81.

   16. 249 U.S. at 52.

   17. 37 *New York University Law Review* 558 (1962).

   18. *Yates v. United States* 354 U.S. 298 (1957) at 339, 343. In contrast with
the conduct ascribed to the defendants in *Yates,* consider the conduct which
Douglas, dissenting with Mr. Justice Black, believed fairly attributed to
Cramer charged with treason for aiding the Germans who came ashore from
a submarine during World War II: in that case, both Justices Douglas and
Black believed, there were treasonable intent and the overt acts of meetings
at which they did "confer, treat and counsel" to aid the enemy. *Cramer v.
United States* 325 U.S. 1 (1945); the Court majority upset the treason convic-
tion.

   19. 360 U.S. 109 (1959).

   20. *Schneider v. State (Irvington Township et al.)* 308 U.S. 147.

   21. *Cantwell v. Connecticut* 310 U.S. 296.

   22. 360 U.S. at 142.

23. 360 U.S. at 144.
24. 360 U.S. at 145-46.
25. 360 U.S. at 153. In dissenting in *Americans for Protection of the Foreign-Born v. Subversive Activities Control Board and Veterans of the Abraham Lincoln Brigade v. Subversive Activities Control Board* 380 U.S. 503, Mr. Justice Black wrote:

> I think that among other things the Act is a bill of attainder; that it imposes cruel, unusual and savage punishments for thought, speech, writing, petition and assembly; and that it stigmatizes people for their beliefs, associations, and views about politics, law and government. The Act has borrowed the worst features of old laws intended to put shackles on the minds and bodies of men, to make them confess to crimes, to make them miserable while in this country and to make it a crime even to attempt to get out of it. It is difficult to find laws more thought-stifling than this one even in countries considered the most benighted. [at 512.]

26. *Gibson v. Florida Legislative Investigation Committee* 372 U.S. 539; Cf. *Scales v. United States* 361 U.S. 952, *Noto v. United States* 361 U.S. 952.
27. 372 U.S. at 559.
28. *Ibid.* at 579.
29. *Brandenburg v. Ohio* 395 U.S. 444 (1969).
30. *Ibid.* at 449-50.
31. 403 U.S. 713 (1971).
32. *Ibid.* at 748.
33. Cf. *Cantwell v. Connecticut* 310 U.S. 296, 307, *Rowan v. Post Office* 397 U.S. 728, 737 (1971).
34. *A Constitutional Faith*, p. 48.
35. *Chaplinsky v. New Hampshire* 315 U.S. 568 (1942): Chaplinsky, a Jehovah's Witness conducting a one-man demonstration, called the town marshal a "damned Fascist" and "damned racketeer."
36. *Beauharnais v. Illinois* 343 U.S. 250 (1952).
37. *Ibid.* at 272.
38. *Ibid.* at 275.
39. 376 U.S. 254 (1964).
40. 379 U.S. 64 (1964).
41. 376 U.S. 279-80.
42. 376 U.S. 293.
43. 379 U.S. 80.
44. 379 U.S. 82.

45. 388 U.S. 130 (1967). The principal cases were *Rosenblatt v. Baer* 383 U.S. 75 (1966), *Associated Press v. Walker* 388 U.S. 130 (1967), *St. Amant v. Thompson* 390 U.S. 727 (1968), *Pickering v. Board of Education* 391 U.S. 563 (1968), *Greenbelt Publishing Co. v. Bresler* 398 U.S. 6 (1970), and *Rosenbloom v. Metromedia, Inc.*, 403 U.S. 29 (1971). In this series of cases the Court extended protections to include criticisms of "public figures" as well as "public officials."

46. 388 U.S. at 162 ff.

47. *Ibid.* at 172–74.

48. 388 U.S. 171–72.

49. *Ginzburg v. Goldwater* 396 U.S. 1049 (1970).

50. *Ibid.*, in *Goldwater v. FCC* 379 U.S. 893 (1964) Mr. Justice Black dissented from denial of review of an equal time application by Senator Goldwater.

51. The adjectives employed by Mr. Justice Brennan in *New York Times v. Sullivan* 376 U.S. at 270.

52. The question whether government may regulate broadcasting so as to assure equal time and fair rejoinder seems as yet unsettled. Mr. Justice Black concurred in *Red Lion Broadcasting Co. v. FCC* and *United States et al. v. RTNDA* 395 U.S. 367, in which the Court, per Mr. Justice White, held constitutional the FCC's application of fairness doctrine. After Mr. Justice Black left the bench, the Court upheld the FCC refusal to order CBS to sell time to two petitioners for "editorial advertising." *CBS v. DNC* 412 U.S. 94 (1973).

53. Note should be taken of special forms of the speaker-audience relationship: in *Saia v. New York* 334 U.S. 558 (1948) and *Kovacs v. Cooper* 336 U.S. 77 (1949) Mr. Justice Black condemned over-broad restrictions on the use of sound-trucks; in *Public Utilities Commission v. Pollak* 343 U.S. 451 (1952) he dissented from allowing Washington city buses to pipe news and "propaganda" to their riders; and in *Talley v. California* 362 U.S. 60 (1960) he wrote the Court's opinion holding void on its face prohibition of anonymous handbills—he called attention to the danger to some writers of being identified and also to the tradition of anonymous pamphleteering, including the publication of *The Federalist*.

54. *Cantwell v. Connecticut* 310 U.S. 296 (1940).

55. *Martin v. Struthers* 319 U.S. 141 (1943).

56. *Terminiello v. Chicago* 337 U.S. 1 (1949).

57. *Kunz v. New York* 340 U.S. 290 (1951).

58. *Cox v. New Hampshire* 312 U.S. 569 (1941).

59. 340 U.S. 315 (1951).

60. *Ibid.* at 326, 328.

61. *Watts v. United States* 394 U.S. 705 (1969).

62. *Ibid.* at 707–08. Cf. 402 F. 2d 676–82 (1968).

63. *United States v. O'Brien* 391 U.S. 367 (1968).

64. *Street v. New York* 394 U.S. 576 (1968).

65. 394 U.S. at 609–10.

66. 319 U.S. 624 (1943). Mr. Justice Black had concurred in the decision to strike down the compulsory flag salute in West Virginia public schools, but the Court's opinion had conceded that "we live by symbols." Symbols unify, but their unifying influence cannot be coercive. Gestures of disrespect for a national symbol surely may be on occasion a more serious form of patriotic concern than a merely ritual deference. One might hope that all would, at least inwardly, "salute" the flag; yet it may be the case that sometimes it is accorded more deference by burning than by receiving mechanical allegiance.

67. 383 U.S. at 516 (1966); *Mishkin v. New York*, dissenting opinion.

68. He did go on to say (516–17), "I wish once more to express my objections to saddling this Court with the irksome and inevitably unpopular and unwholesome task of finally deciding by a case-by-case sight-by-sight personal judgment of the members of this Court what pornography (whatever that means) is too hard core for people to see or read."

69. *Ginsberg v. New York* 390 U.S. 629.

70. *Ibid.* at 46.

71. *Roth v. United States* 354 U.S. 476 (1957).

72. *Chaplinsky v. New Hampshire* 315 U.S. 568.

73. 354 U.S. at 509.

74. *Memoirs v. Massachusetts* 383 U.S. 413 (1966).

75. *Mishkin v. New York* 383 U.S. 502 (1966).

76. *Ginzburg v. United States* 383 U.S. 463 (1966).

77. 383 U.S. 476, 483.

78. *Paris Adult Theater v. Slaton* 413 U.S. 49 ff. (1973).

79. *Ibid.* at 467 ff.

80. *Ibid.* at 475.

81. 383 U.S. 481–82.

82. 383 U.S. at 516.

83. Cf. *A Constitutional Faith*, pp. 53–63.

84. *Hague v. CIO* 307 U.S. 496 (1939).

85. *Ibid.* 515–16.

86. *Thornhill v. Alabama* 310 U.S. 88 (1940).

87. *A Constitutional Faith*, p. 57.

88. *Giboney et al. v. Empire Storage & Ice Co.* 336 U.S. 490 (1949).

89. *NLRB v. Fruit and Vegetable Packers and Warehousement* 377 U.S. 58

(1964); concurring with Mr. Justice Breenan's opinion that secondary picketing of retail stores to persuade customers to cease buying product of primary
employer is not an unfair labor practice, Mr. Justice Black wrote separately
that "to forbid the striking employees of one business to picket the premises
of a neutral business where the purpose of the picketing is to persuade
customers of the neutral business not to buy goods supplied by the struck
company . . . abridges the freedom of speech and press in violation of the
First Amendment." The *Giboney* ruling, he went on, had made it clear that
"because picketing includes patrolling . . . neither *Thornhill* nor the cases that
followed it lend support to the contention that peaceful picketing is beyond
legislative control"; and in such cases "weighing" of First Amendment and
other values is in order. But in the present case, he concluded, the statute
intended "to prevent dissemination of information about the facts of a labor
dispute" and was not aimed at protecting traffic, promoting convenience or
avoiding violence; the aim was "outlawing free discussion of one side of a
certain kind of labor dispute," and it was not enough to say that other
avenues of expression were open. "First Amendment freedoms," he said,
"can no more validly be taken away by degrees than by one fell swoop." 377
U.S. 78–80.

    90. *Cox v. Louisiana* 379 U.S. 536 (1964).

    91. *Brown v. Louisiana* 383 U.S. 131 (1966).

    92. *Edwards v. South Carolina* 372 U.S. 229 (1963).

    93. *Adderley v. Florida* 385 U.S. 39 (1966).

    94. *Walker v. Birmingham* 388 U.S. 507 (1967) and *Shuttlesworth v. Birming-
ham* 394 U.S. 147 (1969).

    95. *Gregory v. Chicago* 394 U.S. 111 (1969).

    96. *Bell v. Maryland* 378 U.S. 226 (1964).

    97. *Amalgamated Food Employees Union v. Logan Valley Plaza* 391 U.S. 308
(1968).

    98. 379 U.S. at 581–84.

    99. 383 U.S. at 151 ff.

    100. 385 U.S. at 46–48.

    101. 378 U.S. at 318, 344–46.

    102. 391 U.S. at 327, 332.

    103. 372 U.S. 229; cf. comment in *Cox v. Louisiana* 379 U.S. at 579.

    104. 394 U.S. 120.

    105. The two cases concerning the Good Friday march of 1963 by Martin
Luther King, Jr. and his associates show the complexity of adjudicating the
demonstration issues. The Court in *Walker*, in 1967, condemned the marchers' failure to challenge the injunction served the day before the march
was scheduled to take place; Mr. Justice Black concurred in the 5–4 decision

upholding the contempt conviction. In *Shuttlesworth*, two years later, the Court unanimously reversed the conviction of the marchers for parading without a permit, Mr. Justice Black concurring in the result. The opinion by Mr. Justice Stewart stressed the open-ended discretion delegated to the City Commissioner to refuse a permit and further asserted that "our decisions have made clear that picketing and parading may constitute methods of expression entitled to First Amendment protection."

Mr. Justice Black's sensitivity to "timeliness" was clearly set forth in *Mills v. Alabama* 384 U.S. 214 (1966).

106. *Tinker v. Des Moines Community School District* 393 U.S. 503 (1968).

107. 393 U.S. at 522; see his tribute to Wesley Sturges for a deeply moving statement of his educational philosophy 72 *Yale Law Jal* 644.

108. 393 U.S. at 522.

109. *United Public Workers v. Mitchell* 330 U.S. 75 (1947).

110. 330 U.S. at 110, 111, 114.

111. *Bond v. Floyd* 385 U.S. 116 (1966).

112. *Bridges v. California, Los Angeles Times-Mirror v. Superior Court* 314 U.S. 252 (1941).

113. *In re Summers* 325 U.S. 561 (1945).

114. *Schware v. Board of Bar Examiners* 353 U.S. 232 (1957).

115. *Konigsberg v. State Bar* 353 U.S. 252 (1957).

116. *In re Anastaplo* 353 U.S. 82 (1957).

117. *Baird v. Arizona* 401 U.S. 1 (1971).

118. *In re Stolar* 401 U.S. 23 (1971).

119. 401 U.S. at 4.

120. *Law Students Civil Rights Research Council v. Wadmond* 401 U.S. 154 (1971).

121. *West Virginia Board of Education v. Barnette* 319 U.S. 624 (1943) reversing *Minersville School District v. Gobitis* 310 U.S. 586 (1940).

122. 319 U.S. 643, 644.

123. *Adler v. Board of Education* 342 U.S. 485 (1952).

124. 342 U.S. at 497.

125. *Keyishian v. Board of Regents* 385 U.S. 589 (1967).

126. 385 U.S. at 620, 628–29.

127. *Griswold v. Connecticut* 381 U.S. 479 (1965).

128. 381 U.S. at 509–10. Mr. Justice Black's strict interpretation of the Fourth Amendment was reflected in his refusal to condemn wire-tapping: *Berger v. New York* 388 U.S. 41 (1967) and *Katz v. United States* 389 U.S. 347 (1967).

129. 385 U.S. 374 (1967).

130. 385 U.S. at 400–01.

131. 385 U.S. at 411 ff.

132. In *Olmstead v. United States* 277 U.S. 438, 478 (1928). In the noted article on privacy in 1890 Brandeis and Warren affirmed the importance of assuring full freedom to discuss public affairs.

133. 385 U.S. at 420. The Court also divided in *Rosenbloom v. Metromedia, Inc.*, a majority, including Mr. Justice Black, affirming public status for a newsstand vendor accused in a radio broadcast of being a "smut-distributor." Two members of the Court contended that he was a private person whose life had been unjustly invaded by the broadcast. Mr. Justice Black appeared to hold the view that what the press makes public *is* public and therefore the content of such expression as is protected by the First Amendment.

134. 376 U.S. 301–02.

135. Quoted in Devol, *Mass Media and the Supreme Court* (New York 1971), at p. 271.

136. *Barenblatt v. United States.*

137. *Konigsberg, Anastaplo, Baird*, and *Stolar*.

138. *Gregory v. Chicago* 394 U.S. 111 (1969). In concurring, Mr. Justice Black wrote: "Speech and press are, of course, to be free, so that public matters can be discussed with impunity. But picketing and demonstrating can be regulated like other conduct of men. I believe that the homes of men, sometimes the last citadel of the tired, weary and the sick, can be protected by government from noisy, tramping, threatening picketers and demonstrators bent on filling the minds of men, women and children with fears of the unknown." (at 125–26).

139. *Stanley v. Georgia* 394 U.S. 557 (1969).

140. 37 *New York University Law Review* (1962) at 559.

141. *Ibid.* at 562.

142. *Everson v. Board of Education* 330 U.S. 1, 18 (1947).

143. *A Constitutional Faith*, p. 46.

144. *Ibid.*, pp. 4, 5.

145. *Engel v. Vitale*, 370 U.S. 421 (1962).

146. *Welsh v. United States* 398 U.S. 333 (1970).

147. *Ibid.* at 337.

148. *Id.*

149. *Ibid.* at 341. Welsh originally had written, "I believe that human life is valuable in and of itself, in its living; therefore I will not injure or kill another human being. This belief . . . is not 'superior' to those arising from any human relation. On the contrary it is essential to every human relation." at 343.

150. *Ibid.* at 342.

151. *Ibid.* at 344.

152. *Ibid.* at 356.

153. *Gillette v. United States* (401 U.S. 437) involved objection to a particular war rather than war in general. Mr. Justice Black concurred in Mr. Justice Marshall's opinion that such an objection, however rooted in conscience, did not fall within authorized exemptions as stipulated by Congress. Mr. Justice Douglas dissented.

154. 35 *New York University Law Review* at 880–81 (1960).

155. 92 S. Ct. 5 (1971).

The First Amendment:
Freedom of Religion

Paul A. Freund

IT IS PARTICULARLY FITTING THAT THESE CEREMONIES BE HELD in Birmingham, for Justice Black dearly loved his native state. I recall a visit he made to the Harvard Law School, where he addressed the Southern Club, an organization of students with some South in their background. (I was invited to attend by a loose construction of the constitution of the club, having grown up in Missouri.) Justice Black urged the students to return to the South after graduation. There are no finer people on earth, he said, than Southerners. "I don't say they are the finest people on earth; I say there are none finer." He went on to suggest that they have one besetting fault: they are too prone to believe in ancestor worship. And so you see that, for all his permissiveness in matters of freedom of religion, even he was ready to mark a limit.

It is fitting, too, that the religious guarantees of the Constitution should form the subject of this concluding session, for Justice Black played a key role in the modern development of those guarantees. He wrote the Court's opinion in the first case—the bus-fare case—declaring that the nonestablishment clause of the First Amendment applied against the states. He wrote the opinion in the first school-prayer case, involving the Regents' prayer in New York. And he helped to change the

Court's position on the flag-salute by changing his own mind
on the issue.

Let me begin by quoting Justice Black's concluding words
in the school bus-fare case, where he spoke for a five-to-four
majority of the Court upholding New Jersey's payment of bus
fares for school children attending parochial as well as public
schools. Justice Black said: "The First Amendment has
erected a wall between church and state. That wall must be
kept high and impregnable. We could not approve the
slightest breach. New Jersey has not breached it here." The
metaphor of the wall was of course taken from the letter of
Thomas Jefferson to the Danbury Baptists. Justice Jackson,
dissenting, thought that between the majority's stern premise
of separation and its permissive conclusion there was an un-
bridged gap in reasoning. "The case which irresistibly comes
to mind as the most fitting precedent," said Justice Jackson, "is
that of Julia who, according to Byron's reports, 'whispering "I
will ne'er consent,"—consented.'" What comes irresistibly to
mind for me in this, as in all the cases involving the principle
of separation of church and state, is rather the passage from
Robert Frost's "Mending Wall":

> "Before I built a wall I'd ask to know
> What I was walling in or walling out,
> And to whom I was like to give offense.
> Something there is that doesn't love a wall,
> That wants it down."

To fathom what we are walling in and walling out in the
religious guarantees of the First Amendment we do well to
start with history. For too often law is history with the history
left out.

The proper relationship of church and state is a problem of
ancient lineage that has long been vexing to governments,

clerics, and citizens. The stage can be set by a passage in the New Testament (for the reference to which I am indebted to the monumental treatise of Canon Stokes on *Church and State in the United States*). A Jewish group tried to bring Paul before the judicial authorities because his teaching seemed to be contrary to Jewish belief. In Acts 18, in the Revised Standard Version, it is recounted:

> But when Paul was about to open his mouth, the deputy Gallio said to the Jews, "If it were a matter of wrong doing or vicious crime, I should have reason to hear with you, O Jews; but since it is a matter of questions about words and names and your own law, see to it yourselves; I refuse to be a judge of these things." And he drove them from the tribunal.

This separation of matters of belief from conduct detrimental to public order, this abstention of the civil authority from help or harm to the mission of religious groups, is, as Canon Stokes observes, an early anticipation of the teaching of Thomas Jefferson.

In the Middle Ages the issue was dramatized by the conflicts of Pope and Emperor. "Render unto Caesar the things that are Caesar's," the Emperor admonished, and by return mail the Pope replied, "And unto God the things that are God's." And how shall the two spheres be marked off, one from the other? This central question was faced by John Locke, whose writings were preeminently influential with the framers of our Constitution, in his *Letter Concerning Toleration*, written probably in 1685 and published in 1689. The passage is worth quoting at some length for its relentless inquiry into the workings of the principle of separation:

> But some may ask, What if the magistrate should enjoin anything by his authority that appears unlawful to the conscience of a private person? I answer, that if government be faithfully administered, and the counsels of the magistrates be

indeed directed to the public good, this will seldom happen. But if, perhaps, it do so fall out, I say, that such a private person is to abstain from the action that he judges unlawful, and he is to undergo the punishment which it is not unlawful for him to bear. For the private judgment of any person concerning a law enacted in political matters, for the public good, does not take away the obligation of that law, nor deserve a dispensation. But if the law indeed be concerning things that lie not within the verge of the magistrate's authority (as for example, that the people, or any party amongst them, should be compelled to embrace a strange religion, and join in the worship and ceremonies of another Church), men are not in these cases obliged by that law, against their consciences. For the political society is instituted for no other end, but only to secure every man's possession of the things of this life...

But what if the magistrate believe such a law as this to be for the public good? I answer: as the private judgment of any particular person, if erroneous, does not exempt him from the obligation of law, so the private judgment (as I may call it) of the magistrate does not give him any new right of imposing laws upon his subjects, which neither was in the constitution of the government granted him, nor ever was in the power of the people to grant, much less if he make it his business to enrich and advance his followers and fellow-secretaries with the spoils of others. But what if the magistrate believe that he has a right to make such laws, and that they are for the public good? And his subjects believe the contrary? Who shall be judge between them? I answer, God alone. For there is no judge upon earth between the supreme magistrate and the people. God, I say, is the only Judge in this case, who will retribute unto every one at the last day according to his deserts; ...

But Americans are too impatient to wait. In the American constitution, for the first time, the principle of separation was embedded in the actual law, so that long before the coming of Locke's day of the last judgment our institutions must interpret the principle and make temporal judgments as best they can in a multitude of puzzling conflicts. The Court has served as a lightning rod, preventing a general conflagration. We have witnessed under the Constitution no kneeling in the snow at Canossa, no murder in the cathedral of Canterbury.

And yet it would be a false romanticism to picture the history of America as a monotonous, cloudless panorama of religious liberty and toleration since the early settlers made the perilous voyage to the new world in search of religious freedom. The names of Anne Hutchinson and Roger Williams, banished from Massachusetts under its Congregational establishment, the exclusion of Quakers and Jesuits from its shores (with a generous exception in case of shipwreck), are sufficient reminders that the early New England colonists, in renouncing the tenets of the mother church in England, did not repudiate all of the church's practices of exclusiveness. The Anglican church itself was established in Virginia and other Southern states. The tolerant regimes of Lord Calvert in Maryland, Roger Williams in Rhode Island, and William Penn in Pennsylvania were notable because they were not typical.

Religious liberty, like so much else in American history, was a function of geographic spaciousness. The colonists were able to set up their own separate theocracies in accordance with their sectarian attachments. At the time of the Federal Constitution only Rhode Island and Virginia (which had only lately disestablished Anglicanism) enjoyed full religious freedom. Six states—New Hampshire, Connecticut, New Jersey, Georgia, North Carolina, and South Carolina—adhered to state-supported religious establishments, and others required attachment to Protestantism for the holding of public office.

How, then, can we explain the libertarianism of the Constitution? For even before the First Amendment was drafted by the first Congress and ratified by the states, the text of the Constitution of 1787 contained a noteworthy guarantee. Article VI provides: "The Senators and Representatives before mentioned, and the members of the several state legislatures, and all executive and judicial officers, both of the United States and of the several States, shall be bound by Oath or Affirmation, to support this Constitution [note the dispensation from the requirement of an oath]; *but no religious test shall ever be required as a qualification to any office or public trust under the United States.*" The latter provision is the only reference to religion in the original Constitution, save for the phrase "in the year of our Lord" in the attestation clause at the end. It would have gone a long way to prevent the preferential establishment of a particular sect on a national scale. But the ratifying conventions in the states were not satisfied with this, and in response to the pressures for a more comprehensive Bill of Rights the first Congress drew up, among other guarantees, the First Amendment.

What were the conditions that impelled the framers, the members of the state ratifying conventions, and the first Congress to be sensitive to the dangers of religious intolerance and a fusion of the secular and the religious, at a time when some form of religious establishment still prevailed in most of the states? A whole series of circumstances seems to have combined to produce this concern.

In the first place, of course, there was a fear of national power. In this view there was no inconsistency between a guarantee against establishment on a national scale and its retention on the state level. Moreover, a multiplicity of sects was developing, and as Madison regarded a multiplicity of secular economic interests as a safeguard against the tyranny of a majority, so a multiplicity of sects was viewed as a protection against any domination by a creedal group. The large numbers of unchurched citizens reinforced this position. Furthermore, the rise of commercial interests made toleration and mutual respect important, as the lords of trade in London had put it in 1750, "to the enriching and improving of a trading

nation." The combination of God and Mammon is an irresist-
ible force. The Revolutionary War, too, had brought a sober-
ing sense of fraternity, especially as Catholic France was an
invaluable ally.

But these worldly spurs were not the only influences prod-
ding the framers. Ideological and philosophical convictions
were strongly at work. The Roger Williams-William Penn
tradition was not forgotten. The Quakers and Baptists were
active, and after all, the Constitutional Convention was held in
the home of Quakerism. This circumstance was borne in on
the members of the convention by an eloquent plea from a
distinguished representative of the New England Baptists, a
spiritual forebear of Justice Black, The Reverend Isaac Backus:

> It has been said by a celebrated writer in politics, that but
> two things were worth contending for,—Religion and Liberty.
> For the latter we are at present nobly exerting ourselves
> through all this extensive continent; and surely no one whose
> bosom feels the patriotic glow in behalf of civil liberty, can
> remain torpid to the more ennobling flame of Religious Free-
> dom.
>
> The free exercises of private judgment, and the unalienable
> rights of conscience, are of too high a rank and dignity to be
> submitted to the decrees of councils, or the imperfect laws of
> fallible legislators. The merciful Father of mankind is the alone
> Lord of conscience. Establishments may be enabled to confer
> worldly distinctions and secular importance. They may make
> hypocrites, but cannot create Christians.

The pronouncement is so startlingly in the style of Justice
Black that one is tempted to charge Isaac Backus with an-
ticipatory plagiarism.

Roger Williams had likewise seen the need for separation in
the vulnerability of the church to political encroachment. The
Garden of the Church, in his figure, must be shielded from
the creeping Wilderness of the State. This was the other side

of the coin of Jefferson's philosophy—that the state should be secured against the political intrusion of the church. And so, philosophically, the religious guarantees were a combination of principles: personal freedom and voluntariness in matters of religion, and a social order in which organized religion and organized politics could lead self-directed lives under a principle of mutual abstention.

Finally, besides these motivations of expediency and of philosophic conviction, there was the influential example of the state of Virginia, which had just enacted Jefferson's long-standing bill for religious liberty, under the leadership of James Madison. Because of their eminence in the national councils, the Virginia experience is of special significance.

In 1784 a bill was introduced to provide for the teaching of the Christian religion, with an assessment on each taxpayer, who could designate the church to which his payment would be applied; and [this is important in appreciating the scope of Madison's opposition] non-Christians would be permitted to designate some other institution of learning as the beneficiary of their payments. Despite this provision for equal treatment of all sectarians and nonsectarians, Madison presented his *Memorial and Remonstrance against Religious Assessments*, which carried the day; the assessment bill was defeated, and Jefferson's bill for religious liberty was enacted: "all men shall be free to profess, and by argument to maintain, their opinion in matters of religion, and that the same shall in no wise diminish, enlarge or affect their civil liberties."

Two conclusions seem to emerge from the Virginia contest: that if Madison is a guide, nonestablishment meant no state financial aid even on a basis of equal treatment, and not simply a guarantee against preferential treatment; and that if Jefferson is a guide, the free exercise of religion meant freedom for believers and nonbelievers alike.

How broad is the privilege of free exercise of religion: does it apply to nonbelievers and how far does it protect conduct based on belief? How sweeping is the nonestablishment guarantee: does it forbid all official aid to religion or only aid that prefers certain sects over others? These questions, which are reasonably clearly answered in the Virginia experience, are still haunting us today under the First and Fourteenth amendments.

The First Amendment, applicable only to the national government, provides: "Congress shall make no law respecting an establishment of religion, or prohibiting the free exercise thereof . . ." Was it intended to be as encompassing in relation to national power as Madison's remonstrance and Jefferson's statute were in relation to Virginia? The evidence on this is sketchy and inconclusive. One item in the progress of the various drafts through Congress is worth special attention: just before the appointment of the conference committee that produced the final version (a committee that included Madison from the House), the Senate refused to concur in a proposal that would have substituted for "establishment of religion" the narrower guarantee "establishment of one religious sect or society in preference to others."

If the precise meaning of the First Amendment is not crystal clear, the application of its safeguards to the states is even more elusive. State establishments continued in New England until the 1830s. In 1868 the Fourteenth Amendment was ratified, providing that no state shall deprive any person of life, liberty, or property without due process of law. To what extent do these words absorb the guarantees of the First Amendment?

A few years later the so-called Blaine Amendment passed the House but failed to secure the necessary two-thirds majority in the Senate. It would have specifically protected the exercise of religion and prohibited a state establishment of religion. But the defeat of this proposal is ambiguous; it may well have been deemed unnecessary in view of the Fourteenth Amendment.

When the "liberty" of the Fourteenth Amendment came to be interpreted in the early twentieth century to include freedom of contract, and then in the 1930s to include freedom of speech, it was no doubt inevitable that it should also be read to include the free exercise of religion. What is not so plain is the inclusion of the nonestablishment safeguard where it is not bound up with free exercise. It is not so plain as a textual matter (is this a matter of "liberty" or "property"), and historically this clause of the First Amendment was addressed peculiarly to the national government, as an aspect of our federal division of powers. Not until the bus-fare case in 1947 did the Supreme Court hold the nonestablishment guarantee to be absorbed into the Fourteenth Amendment equally with the free exercise of religion.

Let me speak briefly about the law of free exercise of religion, the law of nonestablishment, and then the dilemmas posed by the confrontation of the two.

The right of free exercise, enshrined though it is, yields to overriding social interests when these are put in jeopardy by religious practices. The religious commitment of the Mormons to plural marriages had to yield to laws against polygamy. The religious tenets of Christian Scientists cannot prevail over vaccination laws. The religious duty of Jehovah's Witnesses to employ their families as distributors of theological tracts was subordinated to child-labor laws.

When the free exercise of religion has been upheld, it has often been done under more general guarantees, of liberty of speech or assembly or freedom to engage in lawful callings. The right to maintain and attend parochial schools, while it is a cardinal safeguard of free exercise of religion, was established along with the right to maintain and attend a private, nonreligious school, as part of a larger liberty to teach and learn.

The flag-salute cases are revealing in this regard. The first case to reach the Court, the *Gobitis* case in 1940, was treated as

presenting a straightforward claim of exemption on the part of
Jehovah's Witnesses as a matter of free exercise of religion; the
compulsory salute was to them a profanation, a bowing before
false gods. The claim of exemption was denied, in an opinion
by Justice Frankfurter that stressed the secular nature of the
ceremony and the propriety of teaching patriotism in the
schools. Only Justice Stone dissented. Soon thereafter, Justice
Douglas indicated that Justice Black was having second
thoughts about the decision. "Why?" Justice Frankfurter
asked, "Has Hugo been re-reading the Constitution?" No,
said Douglas, but he has been reading the newspapers. At first
blush this reply looks shockingly close to Mr. Dooley on the
Supreme Court. But what Justice Black was reading was not
the election returns, and not merely the widespread editorial
criticism of the *Gobitis* decision. He was presumably reading
the poignant accounts of how the children of Jehovah's Witnesses were ostracized and hounded for objecting to the flag
salute and in some cases expelled from school for not participating. This experience was not irrelevant to the constitutional issue. School children were suffering official penalties
rather than professing a creed in which they did not believe.

When the issue again came before the Court, it was treated
in this larger context. The First Amendment's guarantee of
freedom of speech, not solely of religion, was held to protect
one from being coerced to say what for him was false. It is no
great wonder that in this context the issue was no longer
doubtful for Justice Black. Of course, you may ask whether by
logical analogy a pupil is entitled to full credit for saying that
the earth is flat, if that is indeed his firm and conscientious
conviction. I suppose that if problems of that sort were to arise
the teacher could always avoid a First Amendment issue by
phrasing the question existentially, in terms of the preponder-
ant scientific opinion,—like requiring tobacco companies to
state "The Surgeon General has determined that smoking is
dangerous to health." In this second flag-salute case, inciden-

tally, the Court was assisted by a brief filed on behalf of a Bill of Rights Committee of the American Bar Association, whose chairman was Douglas Arant of the Birmingham bar.

I was making the point that claims under the free exercise clause are sometimes upheld under a more general guarantee of liberty. But it is not always so. The Amish sect, believing that book learning beyond the rudiments of a grammar-school education promotes the work of the devil, refused to send their children to school beyond that stage, thereby running afoul of the compulsory schooling law. In a decision that surely goes to the verge of the law, the Amish were sustained in their position. The decision is hardly likely to serve as a precedent beyond its special facts—the Amish communities are self-contained and self-sufficient, neither a drain on, nor a hazard to, the general population. Can the religious concerns of the nonconformist be accommodated without undue disruption of important social concerns of the state—this form of question, imprecise as it is, seems as close as we can get to a sovereign formula for resolving issues of the free exercise of religion.

How does this formula work? Let me consider two cases involving the claims of Sabbatarians—Seventh-Day Adventists or Orthodox Jews. First, the case of claims to unemployment benefits even though the religious observances of the claimants preclude their accepting employment on Saturdays. The inability to work on that one day and the limited numbers involved were not so serious a threat to the functioning of the unemployment insurance system as to warrant an overriding of the religious nonconformity. (Of course, if a sect were to emerge that believed passionately that we were divinely ordered to labor just two days a week, the outcome would not necessarily be the same. Of such practical accommodations and distinctions is constitutional law made.) The second case is that of Sabbatarians claiming an exemption from Sunday-closing laws because their religion forbids them to keep their shops open on Saturday and the law would force them to close for a second day in the week. But the secular aim of the law—a uniform day of rest—was thought by a majority of the Court to be threatened if an exemption were required. The conclusion is surely weakened by the fact that the Sunday laws themselves are riddled with statutory exemptions.

A final example on the question of accommodating the religious nonconformist is the conscientious objector to war on a selective basis, the believer in the Thomistic doctrine of the just and the unjust war. The unjust war is one in which the good to be achieved is outweighed by the moral costs, a disproportion of means to ends that marks the whole enterprise as immoral. But this calculus is essentially the same as that undertaken by a political critic of a particular war, and so an exemption on this ground would run the risk of undermining the system of compulsory service, unless lines could be drawn on the basis of intensity of feelings of repugnance toward the war. This analysis may help to explain, if not to justify, the Court's decision that conscientious objection to a particular war did not qualify a draftee for exemption.

The conscientious religious objector to a war was thus in a favored position—vis-à-vis the Thomist, and apparently vis-à-vis the conscientious objector on nonreligious but moral grounds. Is not this preference a violation of the nonestablishment clause? The Court skirted the issue as to nonreligious objections by giving religion a broad meaning in this context, adopting a view of religious belief that includes those ultimate concerns (in Tillich's term) that serve the function in one person's life that traditional Theistic religion serves in other lives. The shadow of a tension begins to appear between the two guarantees—recognition of free-exercise claims may verge on establishment of religion.

Let me turn more particularly to the nonestablishment guarantee. Not even a Justice Black, I believe, for all his resourceful literalism in reading the Bill of Rights, could find the answers to the puzzles by turning to the text. The two clauses,

I have said, are on occasion in tension. May, for example, G.I. benefits be applied to pay tuition at a divinity school, no less than at a dental or dancing school? Is this an application of public funds to promote the teaching of religion, or is it the free exercise of religion by the veteran himself?

In fact, the key word in the two clauses, "religion," has a different meaning in each clause. If Jehovah's Witnesses are entitled to exemption from the flag salute because for them it is a religious exercise, why must it not be banned in the public schools as an establishment of religion? The answer is that for purposes of free exercise religion is defined by the nonconformist, but for purposes of establishment it is defined by the dominant consensus.

Many of the modern controversies, like those in Virginia in Jefferson's time, center on public aid to church-related schools. Some commentators, taking their cue from the bus-fare case, profess to find the key to judgment in whether the state aid is a benefit to the child or to the school. Of course it is both. This test resembles the early nineteenth-century effort to decide questions of state regulation of interstate business by characterizing the state law (for example, a quarantine on incoming steamboat passengers or a pilotage requirement) as either a regulation of commerce, and so invalid, or a protection of local safety, health, or welfare, and so valid. The beginning of wisdom came when it was recognized that the law was both, and that a fair accommodation between the two needs had to be sought.

Our present constitutional law on the subject of religious establishment has been notably advanced by Chief Justice Burger in a series of opinions on public aid. He has set forth a threefold guide (the term test is too deceptively mechanical), whereby the Court looks at the primary purpose of the aid, whether to advance religion or to promote a secular end; at the dominant effect of the aid; and at the degree of entanglement of church and state that the law would entail. This last factor

is especially significant, and it is historically authentic: the
Garden and the Wilderness must not become intertwined.

When the guidelines are applied, the answers are not self-
evident, nor is there a tidy pattern that has been laid out.
Some public services that reach schoolchildren wherever they
are and are nonideological, like nursing programs and hot
lunches, are quite clearly valid. The loan of secular textbooks
has also been upheld, though in view of later decisions this one
is hard to reconcile. Outright unconditional grants to parochial schools would be illegitimate; what then of grants for
limited (secular) purposes, like the teaching of science or lan-
guages? In light of the insistence by many supporters of
church-related schools that education is indivisible and the
religious (or nonreligious) character of the institution per-
meates all instruction, it would be necessary at best to engage
in surveillance of parochial schools to assess the nature of
instruction in so-called secular subjects. Thus the schools are
impaled on a dilemma: either the aid is too undifferentiated or
it requires supervision—entanglement—to try to identify the
religious and the secular components. What then of tax deductions to parents for tuition payments at parochial schools? The
element of surveillance is avoided, but, as a majority of the
Court held, the other horn of the dilemma is not escaped, for
in economic terms the tax benefit is not essentially different
from an unconditional grant to the schools. Perhaps if the tax
deduction were more general, covering (up to a certain
maximum) any educational expenses, including the cost of
private lessons in music, or in tennis, or in a foreign language,
the benefit would be so diffused that the church-state issue
would be de-fused, as in the case of tax deductions for all
charitable contributions, including religious ones. No one can
safely predict the outcome, save that the Court would be divided.

Some of the specific controversies may seem trivial when
looked at in isolation. The real contest has been one between

two Latin maxims: *de minimis non curat lex* (the law is not concerned with trifles) and *obsta principiis* (withstand beginnings, beware the entering wedge). The latter maxim has prevailed, as it did in Madison's Remonstrance in Virginia.

If puzzles and even apparent inconsistencies emerge, we must remember that the churches themselves have not escaped these pitfalls in their own positions. Protestant and Jewish groups that oppose public aid to parochial schools are not averse to receiving the benefit of tax exemption for their churches and synagogues. And, as Father Drinan asks in an exceedingly thoughtful study, *Religion, the Courts, and Public Policy,* ". . . can Catholics have it both ways—urging the secularization of the public schools when arguing for tax support for parochial schools and encouraging the communication of religious and theistic values when dealing with the mission of the public school?"

I should like to close, for the sake of illustration, with a more extended analysis of one current issue that will not down—the school prayer cases. To the middle of the nineteenth century elementary education was largely in the hands of sectarian schools. When the public-school movement came to fruition, a residue was left in the form of less sectarian, but broadly Protestant, religious observances, against which Catholics were the chief objectors. Some further concession was made in certain states, by granting exemptions to objectors.

The Regents' prayer in New York was an effort to enlarge pan-Protestantism and pan-Christianity to pan-religion, through a kind of to-whom-it-may-concern prayer. The decisions upsetting this and other forms of prayer in unison, including the Lord's Prayer observance, have raised a number of anxious questions in thoughtful minds, and to these I shall try to address myself.

First. Don't the decisions actually interfere with the free exercise of religion by the majority? This way of putting the issue really begs the question. The free exercise of religion, it is said, includes the right to worship in one's accustomed way. But does it follow that where a majority in a school are Jews or Catholics they may bring in a rabbi or priest to conduct full-scale religious services every day, with a full panoply of ritual and insignia, giving the minority the privilege of absenting themselves? No one, I assume, would uphold such a free exercise of religion by the majority. The proper setting for such a free exercise would be a parochial school, the maintenance of which is guaranteed under the Constitution.

But, it may be argued, at least a nonsectarian exercise should be permitted. With more than two hundred-odd sects in the United States, over eighty of them having more than fifty thousand members each, it is not easy to envisage a strictly nonsectarian religious exercise. One man's piety is another's idolatry. Moreover, to make the secular courts the arbiter of what is permitted as nonsectarian religion and what is prohibited as sectarian would compound the intrusion of the secular arm into the religious sphere. This was the point of the case some years ago holding that the motion picture "The Miracle" could not be banned in New York under a law forbidding "sacrilegious" pictures.

When the "Miracle" case was decided by the Supreme Court, *The Pilot*, the publication of the Boston Archdiocese, expressed its approval, in a thoughtful editorial. "For some strange reason," *The Pilot* said, "the impression has got about that Catholics are uniformly unhappy about the recent ruling of the Supreme Court on the occasion of 'The Miracle' case. This simply is not so. . . . The Supreme Court merely indicated its incapacity to define an essentially theological term— sacrilegious. No one should be surprised that a group of jurists exercising a civil function in a pluralistic society should refrain from such a definition."

The real choice before the Court in the school cases was whether to draw the line among prayers, upholding some and rejecting others, or to draw the line between all devotional exercises on the one hand and objective studies of a literary or historical kind of the other. Considering the functions of a civil court, no one should be surprised that the line was drawn in the latter way.

Second. Isn't the minority given sufficient protection by being excused from participation? The key to this aspect of the case is the fact that the exercises took place in a school during the school day. The psychological constraint to conform is strong in this atmosphere, and nonconformity produces a stigma that is real and painful to a child. As Justice Frankfurter put it in the released-time case:

> That a child is offered an alternative may reduce the constraint; it does not eliminate the operation of influence by the school in matters sacred to conscience and outside the school's domain. The law of imitation operates, and non-conformity is not an outstanding characteristic of children. The result is an obvious pressure upon children to attend.

Why, then, it may be asked, were Jehovah's Witnesses thought to be adequately protected in their conscience by being granted exemption from the flag salute, without abolishing the ceremony altogether from the schools? The answer is that the flag salute is, by general assent, regarded as a nonreligious exercise; a sect, however, which regards it as an affront to religious commands may be excused from compliance.

The question of excuse or exemption can be viewed on a spectrum of public regulations or practices. At one end are the clearly sectarian exercises, such as a full-scale religious service in the classroom. Exemption would hardly be thought adequate relief for the dissenters. For reasons which I have already suggested, all clearly religious exercises have now been put in this category. Next come exercises like the flag salute, which to some carry a religious connotation. Finally, at

the other end of the spectrum, are such secular rules as those
forbidding polygamy, rules which a certain religious sect finds
in conflict with its religious duties. Here not even exemption
is granted, in view of the social imperative of the civil rule.
The same would be true, I have no doubt, if a sect protested
that to pay taxes is sinful. In short, a solution by way of
exempting the religious dissenter is not a sovereign remedy; in
some circumstances it is too little, in others it may be too
generous.

Third. Do the prayer decisions threaten other civic practices which in some way involve religion with the state? What,
for example, is the legal status of chaplains in Congress, in the
armed services, or in prisons? The opinions are at pains to
point out that the decision is addressed to religious exercises in
the public schools and is not to be taken in any doctrinaire way
as a barrier to every civil program that in some way involves
religion.

From the standpoint of constraint on the individual, an
opening prayer in Congress is surely distinguishable from the
prayer exercise in the schoolroom. And chaplains in the armed
services or in prisons may be a means of preserving the free
exercise of religion for those whom the government has dis-
placed from their normal places of worship. Similarly with
G.I. benefits that can be used to pay tuition at a theological
school; if the money can be used for dental or dancing school,
there would be a question of denial of free exercise of religion
to forbid its use at a divinity school. In these examples, the
guarantee against establishment runs into the countervailing
guarantee of free exercise. In the school prayer cases these two
branches of the First Amendment point harmoniously in one
direction.

Fourth. Does not the decision ignore the rightful place of
moral education in the public schools? Is this the time to
weaken our all too fragile defenses against moral coarseness
and delinquency? The question sounds more horrendous than

it should. It ignores the essential role of the home and the place of worship in the full education of the child. Moreover, it assumes that there is some irreplaceable value in a prescribed prayer or ritual Bible reading as a means of moral education. Such an assumption is surely a dubious one. A school prayer at best would face the dilemma of being so bland as to be meaningless or so sectarian as to be divisive and to some repelling. An English cleric recently questioned the value of a religious assembly in the schools, saying, "The whole idea presented is of God as a trivial inconvenience that must be got out of the way before getting down to the real work of the day."

But the question of the loss to education is not whether the prayer exercise has some value. Even if it has, the question is rather whether this avowedly religious exercise is an irreplaceable or unique mode of strengthening the moral aspect of education. What, in other words, is there to take its place?

At least three lines of development can be followed (aside, of course, from greater emphasis on the home and the place of worship).

The first, closest to the prayer itself, is the brief period of silent reverence or meditation, during which each pupil will recite to himself what his heart or his up-bringing may prompt.

The second mode of moral education is curricular. It might include an exercise in which pupils are individually asked to select and read passages of moral instruction from whatever source. But all such brief inspirational exercises appear weak in comparison with more thoroughgoing efforts to build moral values into a course of study. The greatest effect of the Court's decision may be, it is hoped, a serious and basic inquiry into the moral component of public education. I would hope that, under the stimulus of the decision, encouragement will be given to those educators who are striving in social studies to teach awareness of moral issues, ways of identifying those issues, and habits of ethical analysis that will endure as part of an individual's mental make-up.

A third approach to moral education—in addition to the special exercise and possible curricular developments—might be called atmospheric. This is a function, above all, of the teacher. Reverence for what we know, humility in the presence of the unknown, awe in the face of the unknowable— these are pervasive moods of the spirit that transcend religious differences and make of learning itself a spiritual adventure. A story of Willard Gibbs, the great Yale scientist, describes him standing before a blackboard on which he had worked out an abstruse equation, tears streaming down his cheeks, and the class staring at the board with the gaze of one who had just seen angels. No Court or Constitution stands in the way of that kind of moral and spiritual experience. All that stands in the way is our indifference or inadequacy to meet the challenge.

Those who complain that the Court has driven God out of the schoolroom are men and women of little faith. To them I would recall the final lines of Wordsworth's great sonnet:

"... Dear child, dear girl, who walkest with me here,
If thou appear untouch'd by solemn thought
Thy nature is not therefore less divine.
Thou liest in Abraham's bosom all the year,
And worshipst at the temple's inner shrine,
God being with thee when we know it not."

Hugo Black was a spiritual son of Roger Williams, Thomas Jefferson, and Isaac Backus, and he stood in an authentic constitutional tradition. So far from being hostile to religion his philosophy was religious in the deepest sense, like that of the author of the Declaration of Independence who could write "all men are created equal" and are "endowed by their Creator with certain inalienable rights." One who believed passionately, as did Justice Black, in these principles was a God-intoxicated man, whatever his formal professions or observances.

Justice Black believed that voluntarism was of the essence of religion. His faith was in the mind and will of ordinary men and women, free individuals, not people in the mass or in the mob. His faith was drawn from the wellsprings of the Republic, and it refreshes us today.

Remarks in a
Clay County Cornfield

Max Lerner

A S YOU HAVE JUST HEARD, I AM NOT THE CHIEF JUSTICE OF
the United States. Nor is my name Burger. In fact, after I
have finished these brief remarks you may decide that my
name is not even Max—that it is anticlimax.*

I come with some anxiety to your lovely little community
as an outsider, in fact a New Yorker, a representative of that
dangerous and endangered species we call New York. In the
hotel elevator this morning back in Birmingham, I met several
people and one of them said, "Are you going to Ashland today?" I said "Yes." He said, "Well, you will find it interesting
but pretty primitive." I said "Well, I am pretty primitive myself. I will find myself at home there." And I must say I do. I
feel at home with my old and new friends of the Black family.
Some of my old friends, Virginia Durr and Josephine Black;
my new friends Elizabeth Black, Graham and Hugo Black,
Jr., and their children, and all of my new friends of Birmingham.

Now I feel at home with you because you have been so very
generous in being willing to have me pinch-hit for the Chief
Justice. But also because I come from a little town not very

*Dr. Lerner made this extemporaneous talk when he was asked to substi-
tute for Chief Justice Burger in dedicating the site of the future Hugo
Black Library in the Justice's home town of Ashland, Alabama.

different from this in another country. My family came over from Russia a long time ago. I was four years old. We came in steerage. We were part of the immigrant groups that came to this country. We didn't have an easy time of it. We had to till hard and stony ground. Like so many Americans, we often found life difficult and tragic. But we believed in the American dream—the dream of possibility, the dream that on this continent life could be made free and equal and good, not just for some but for all.

I would like to think with Harold Laski, who was one of the leaders of the British Labor Party when he said, "When the leaders of the people ask their followers to die for a dream, they have a right to know in whose behalf the dream is being dreamt."

The dream *is* being dreamt. We really have a great country. Here is a dream of possibility: how life can be lived, not just by some privileged few but by all.

I don't know how Hugo Black knew this. I know he knew Harold Laski. I remember that when he went to Europe with Josephine, he was in London visiting with Harold Laski. He was buying some books there in London. As a matter of fact, my friend Virginia Hamilton, who wrote that quite brilliant, wonderful book *Hugo Black, The Alabama Years*, mentions that incident of Laski and Hugo in London buying some books together. You see I didn't know whether Hugo Black was moved by this particular sentence of Laski's, but I do know that he held the dream to be real and summed up in that phrase, "in whose behalf is the dream dreamt?"

So for several days in Birmingham we have talked about Justice Black and the Bill of Rights. Some of our language has been very erudite, very legal, very technical. Yet what came through was his friendliness and especially his passion for freedom.

You know that freedom is very crucial. But there is another aspect of freedom. It is *freedom for what?* We want to be free, but we want to be free so that we can do something to improve the quality of life in our country. Not only did Justice Black have a passion for freedom; he had a passion for equality. He had a passion to make sure that we would not forget that dream, dreamt not just in behalf of some but in behalf of all.

Now I don't want to get into our today's politics, but I have to say one thing. Men go around our country today telling us that they care about us, that they care about *you*—what happens to *you*. But you know, I sometimes wonder about at least some of them, whether they are telling the truth. Whether they really care. But really, you know, Hugo Black *did* care. I suspect that one reason he cared for this town was that he was born and grew up in this town of Ashland; he remembered the general store that his family kept, the post office they lived in, the little three-room Ashland Academy, and that little law office over a store where he hung his shingle—the little law office that burned down. And I don't think that he could have cared so passionately as he did about people if he had not had his roots among the people here in Ashland.

One of the Greek myths tells about a giant called Antaeus. If you could lift him off the ground, you could crush him in spite of his strength. But if he could touch the earth, if he could kiss the earth, his mother, he was invincible. I would myself say this about Hugo Black: The reason he was so strong was that he never left, in a deep way, this little town. He was always in touch with the earth, his mother. Physically he did leave, because a man has to leave to go out into the world. He learned much of what he loved about the nation in that great world. But he never in spirit left this town.

May I say that there was a period when Alabama left Hugo Black and when Ashland as well left Hugo Black. But we can understand why that was. I think it was particularly true after the school desegregation decision, the *Brown* decision. But the wonderful thing is that Alabama and Ashland came back to him.

And he came back to Ashland. It is a lovely completed circle. At first Ashland gave Hugo Black to the nation. By planning and I hope by completing this Hugo Black Memorial you are keeping him in your own community again.

There were some things for which Hugo Black had a passion. He cared passionately about our country and its people. And he cared passionately about books and ideas and what ideas could do and what books could mean, not only for intellectuals and writers, but also for all people, for all of us.

So it is fitting and proper that we should dedicate this library to his name. His name will live longer for its books that he loved will live longer, and so will the country that he loved.

INDEX

HUGO BLACK AND THE BILL OF RIGHTS
was composed in VIP Janson by
The Composing Room, Grand Rapids, Michigan,
printed by Thomson-Shore, Inc., Dexter, Michigan
and bound by John H. Dekker & Sons, Grand Rapids, Michigan.
Production: Paul R. Kennedy
Book Design: Anna F. Jacobs